DIANE ACKERMAN
Deep Play

Poet, essayist, and naturalist, Diane Ackerman was born in Waukegan, Illinois. She received an M.A., M.F.A., and Ph.D. from Cornell University. Her poetry has been published in many leading literary journals, and in the books *The Planets: A Cosmic Pastoral*; *Wife of Light*; *Lady Faustus*; *Reverse Thunder: A Dramatic Poem*; *Jaguar of Sweet Laughter: New And Selected Poems*; and *I Praise My Destroyer*. Her works of nonfiction include *Deep Play*; *A Slender Thread*; *The Rarest of the Rare*; *A Natural History of Love*; *The Moon by Whale Light and Other Adventures Among Bats, Crocodilians, Penguins, and Whales*; *A Natural History of the Senses*; and *On Extended Wings*, a memoir of flying. Her bestselling *A Natural History of the Senses* was the basis for a PBS television series, *Mystery of the Senses*, in which she was featured as host and narrator. She is also writing a series of books for children, the first two of which are *Monk Seal Hideaway* and *Bats: Shadows in the Night*, and she is co-editor, with Jeanne Mackin, of an anthology, *The Book of Love*.

Ms. Ackerman has received the Academy of American Poets' Lavan Award, and grants from the National Endowment for the Arts and the Rockefeller Foundation, among other recognitions. Honored as a Literary Lion by the New York Public Library, she has taught at several universities, including Columbia, Cornell, William & Mary, and Ohio University. Her essays about nature and human nature have appeared in *National Geographic*, *The New Yorker*, *The New York Times*, *Parade*, and other journals.

Deep Play

DIANE ACKERMAN

Deep Play

Illustrations by Peter Sis

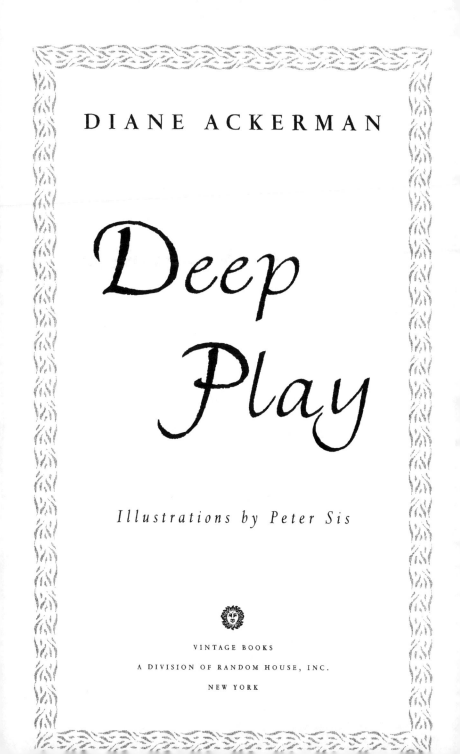

VINTAGE BOOKS

A DIVISION OF RANDOM HOUSE, INC.

NEW YORK

Grateful acknowledgment is made to the following for permission to reprint previously published material:

Farrar, Straus & Giroux, Inc.: Brief excerpts from "A Native Hill" and "The Body and the Earth" from *Recollected Essays, 1965–1980* by Wendell Berry. Copyright © 1981 by Wendell Berry. Reprinted by permission of North Point Press, a division of Farrar, Straus & Giroux, Inc.

Henry Holt and Company, Inc. and Random House UK: Eight lines from "Two Tramps in Mud Time" from *The Poetry of Robert Frost* edited by Edward Connery Lathem. Copyright © 1936 by Robert Frost. Copyright © 1964 by Lesley Frost Ballantine. Copyright © 1969 by Henry Holt & Company. Rights throughout the British Commonwealth are controlled by Random House UK. Reprinted by permission of Henry Holt and Company, Inc., and Random House UK.

International Work Group for Indigenous Affairs: Excerpt from Document 54, "Land Rights Now" by Gulawarrwuy Yunupingu and Silas Roberts. Reprinted by permission of International Work Group for Indigenous Affairs, Copenhagen, Denmark.

Brother Joseph Keenan: Excerpt from "The Art of Taking Tea" by Brother Joseph Keenan. Reprinted by permission.

Alfred A. Knopf, Inc.: Excerpt from pg. 109 of *Lyrical and Critical Essays* by Albert Camus, translated by Ellen Conroy Kennedy. Copyright © 1968 by Alfred A. Knopf, Inc. Reprinted by permission of the publisher.

New Directions Publishing Corporation and David Higham Associates Limited: Three lines from "Fern Hill" from *The Poems of Dylan Thomas*. Copyright © 1945 by The Trustees for the copyrights of Dylan Thomas. Rights throughout the world, excluding the United States, are controlled by David Higham Associates Limited. Reprinted by permission of New Directions Publishing Corporation and David Higham Associates Limited.

Random House, Inc.: "School Prayer" from *I Praise My Destroyer* by Diane Ackerman. Copyright © 1998 by Diane Ackerman. Reprinted by permission of Random House, Inc.

Vintage and colophon are registered trademarks of Random House, Inc.

The Library of Congress cataloged the Random House edition as follows:
Ackerman, Diane.
Deep play / Diane Ackerman. — 1st ed.
p. cm.
Includes bibliographical references and index.
1. Play—Psychological aspects. I. Title.
BF717.A23 1999
128—dc21 98-35067

Vintage ISBN: 978-0-679-77135-7

www.vintagebooks.com

. . . man is made God's plaything, and that is the best part of him. Therefore every man and woman should live life accordingly, and play the noblest games. . . . What, then, is the right way of living? Life must be lived as play . . .

—Plato, *Laws*

Preface

*A*ll alone at the rim of the known world, they stood like brightly uniformed sentinels and stared out to sea. What did they watch for across the windswept white deserts and galloping tar-blue waves? What signposts did they remember that would guide

them home after a long oceanic wandering? A certain shade of bay water, a dialect of current, a familiar arpeggio of ice-glazed rock? Returning to a thousandfold teeming mass of penguins, did they recognize the relief map of a spouse's face? Did they dream? What are penguin dreams? Food and famine, ice floes, lunging leopard seals?

Standing in the blustery Antarctic wind, while a vast city-state of penguins milled noisily around me, I was surprised by everything—the number of penguins, whose raucous calls blurred into a symphonic screech; the brutality of the cold biting through my jacket; the way my mind obsessed about how penguins view life; the unexpected voluptuousness of the vista. I had always imagined them living among ice palaces in windswept rookeries of monotone white, but I discovered that their world danced with minute prisms. More colorful than a rain forest, snow's never-ending white contains all colors, could we but see them. And in such extreme cold one can, which I learned with the force of a revelation. Because the surgical winds were blowing sharp as a scalpel, clouds couldn't form in the frigid air. But suddenly, out of the brilliant blue emptiness, snow began falling in a confetti-sparkle of diamond dust. I was standing inside a kaleidoscope. What did those emperor penguins make of it? I wondered. Or of me, for that matter. After all, their world was half the man-devils' and half their own. Clothed in brilliant red parkas, spawned from the sides of a colossal metal fish that floated upon the water, my shipmates and I had arrived to stalk without killing, while gabbling among ourselves, sometimes clicking and clacking—tall gangly creatures who stomped slowly through snow and never slid downhill on our bellies, or used beaks as ice picks when climbing a steep slope, or swam fast after catapulting into the sea. We were baritone beings who dragged, drove, wore, and carried an endless array of things. I felt ashamed of my belongings—some objects for survival, but others merely for a sense of connectedness to the known world, a symbolic trail to my past. As my sense of identity began to seep out of me and extend itself to the penguins, I realized that they were the ultimate ascetics, creatures that possessed nothing, nested with nothing, traded nothing, carried nothing but their young.

Far from home, extravagantly unencumbered, they reminded me of the colorful thrall I'd left behind—cities and temptations, a carnival of possessions, blooming landscapes, family cares and errands, the elaborate rules of social dressage. Perhaps that's why I found myself free-associating in homely comparisons. They looked formal as waiters, or ceremonial as a village of totem poles, or they did a Chaplinesque walk, or glowed like Hopi kachinas carved to symbolize the soul of the wilderness. I did not find them human, I knew they did not choose to be stately, deliberate, and imposing. They stood doll-like, their legs set close to their tails; they were upright by design, growing large and burly enough to dive deep through frigid waters to feast on squid. Letting my mind spin on into caricature, I fancied them monarchs of all they surveyed, riding ice-floe coaches, and wearing a royal purple that came, not from sea snails, but from the atmosphere itself, when the cloak of night descended over them.

Untethered, my mind roamed the ice floes for hours, devouring each moment, far from any trace of past or future, unacquainted with my body, light as diamond dust. My gaze slid easily from the ice beneath the penguins' feet up their torpedo-shaped bodies, where pale lemon shirtfronts grade to sunrise gold at the neck, around their orange-gold crowns and lilac bills, then at last up to the star-encrusted heavens. Their ways may be mucky and bird-physical, but a saintly aura clung to them. Perhaps it was their vigil in that harsh desert. Living beacons, they brought life to a desolate part of the planet, and reminded me how rugged, how durable life is. Life that can evolve around volcanic lips in the deepest sea trenches. Life that can thrive on mountaintops high

as the jet stream. Life that endures with grace even at the ends of
the earth. For emperors never touch land. They live out their
lives standing sentry on shelf ice. For hours I stood watching
them as hypnotically as they watched the sea, wholly absorbed
by their starch and vitality. Haloed in blue, they carried the sky
on their shoulders. They alone seemed to connect the earth and
night.

For the most part, the details of that new world recorded
themselves on my senses. When thought happened, it bedeviled
me. Why did penguins so fascinate me that I had studied them
exhaustively in books, raised baby penguins in a seaquarium,
traveled the length of a continent, survived physical hardships,
and sailed over staggering oceans just to witness them and their
dazzlingly remote landscape? I was intrigued by their protective
zeal. They are such devoted parents that they will even pick up
frozen or ruined eggs and try to incubate them—or try to incubate stones, or an old dead chick. Committed, self-sacrificing, they
brave raging blizzards and ocean hazards in stultifying cold to
fledge one fluffy, owl-faced chick. I was beguiled by the thought
of hot-blooded beings ruling a world of ice, which they had
adapted to in ingenious ways. Without their inner campfires, emperors would freeze to rubble. Yet cold didn't seem to bother
them as much as heat. Toasty underneath thick layers of blubber,
watertight and airtight, they lived inside feather comforters they
could never toss aside. At the coldest spot on earth, scoured by
200 mph winds and temperatures falling toward −100°F, how
odd to see penguins battle heatstroke by blushing, panting,
ruffling their feathers, lying on their bellies, exposing their
underarms. I was captivated by the rare, altogether-in-the-
raw, availability of emperors. No animal is more vulnerable,
more open to life's vicissitudes and the roughest weathers. Wholly
visible on the shelf ice, they did not fly away like the forest or jun-
gle birds I had known, which quickly became silhouettes in the

tree canopy, destined to be studied one glimpse at a time. I was dumbfounded by how beautifully the emperors flew in water—fluent, streamlined, magnificently aquatic—gliding through realms I could only guess at. Above all, they enchanted me because they were still feathered mysteries.

If someone had broken the spell of that magical day, I could easily have given my name and other particulars, but I would only gradually have emerged into my familiar world. It would have felt like surfacing from a deep-sea dive, or landing on earth after a week in orbit. I could have moved quickly and decisively if I needed to—if anything, I felt stronger than usual, more adroit, better informed. I knew and abided by the rules of the game I was playing—the weather and animal rules, the time rules, the danger rules, the social rules with my shipmates. I was alert but also ecstatic. My mood was a combination of clarity, wild enthusiasm, saturation in the moment, and wonder. In that waking trance, I was enjoying a thrilling form of play, one I've come to relish throughout my life, and have often chronicled in my books. Over the years, I've become increasingly aware of what play, and especially deep play, has meant to me, to all of us. We long for its heights, which some people often visit and others must learn to find, but everyone experiences as replenishing. Opportunities for deep play abound. In its thrall we become ideal versions of ourselves. Deep play has been such an important part of my life that I've decided to explore some of its lessons and mysteries. I begin by looking first at play in general and how it has shaped us as human beings, and then at deep play, whose many moods and varieties help to define who we are and all we wish to be.

Contents

Deep Play

CHAPTER ONE

Deep Play

Deep. *adj.* **1.** The most intense or extreme part. **2.** Profoundly absorbed or immersed. **3.** A distance estimated in fathoms.

—*The American Heritage Dictionary of the English Language*, 3rd edition

PLAY. It is an activity which proceeds within certain limits of time and space, in a visible order, according to rules freely accepted, and outside the sphere of necessity or material utility. The play-mood is one of rapture and enthusiasm, and is sacred or festive in accordance with the occasion. A feeling of exaltation and tension accompanies the action.

—Johan Huizinga, *Homo Ludens*

*E*veryone understands play. If I were in the park, and a girl invited me to play beanbag toss, she might well get bored if I seemed clumsy and slow—just as a dog playing fetch might get bored and go looking for better company. But why play at all? Every element of the human saga requires play. We evolved through play. Our culture thrives on play. Courtship includes high theater, rituals, and ceremonies of play. Ideas are playful reverberations of the mind. Language is a playing with words until they can impersonate physical objects and abstract ideas.

Animal play serves many purposes. It can be a dress rehearsal for adult life, as when young mammals play courtship games, war games, socializing games, motor-skills games. Monk-seal pups playing rough-and-tumble in the surf and tiger cubs pouncing on one another in mock battle are perfecting techniques that will save their lives. Play is far older than humans. It's so familiar to us, so deeply ingrained in the matrix of our childhood, that we take it for granted. But consider this: ants don't play. They don't need to. Programmed for certain behaviors, they automatically perform them from birth. Learning through repetition, honed skills, and ingenuity isn't required in their heritage. The more an animal needs to learn in order to survive, the more it needs to play. The more leisure time it has, the more it can play. Do some higher animals—dolphins, chimpanzees—play with us because they're intelligent beings blessed with leisure time, or because they're playful in the same way tiger cubs are? For all we know, what we call *intelligence* may be a characteristic exclusively of primates. It may not be life's pinnacle at all, but simply one mode of *knowing,* one we happen to master and cherish. Play is widespread among animals because it invites problem-solving, allowing a creature to test its limits and develop strategies. In a dangerous world, where dramas change daily, survival belongs to the agile not the idle. We may think of play as optional, a casual activity. But play is fundamental to evolution. Without play, humans and many other animals would perish.

Animals play, in part, to stay active and fit. The exploring play of primates helps them gather information about their environment and food sources. The escape play of horses keeps them in shape for flight. Social play establishes rank, mate-finding, and cooperation when needed. Play probably helps to keep an animal's senses well informed and alert. The central nervous system needs a certain amount of stimulation. To a dynamic organism, monotony is unbearable. Young animals don't know what is important, what can be safely ignored; they have had fewer novel experiences, and their senses are fresh and highly sensitive. Everything matters.

Even crows play. When I'm out biking, I often see crows wearing plastic wing tags installed by researchers at the nearby ornithology lab. Do those colorful epaulets confer special status in the crow community, I wonder? But it does make them easier to study, and researchers have learned that crows are extraordinarily sociable and devoted to family. Five years' worth of offspring may help out around their parents' home nest during breeding season. When they mate, they nest close to home and are lifelong spouses. They help raise nieces and nephews, they often hunt with others, and they play all sorts of games. Two young crows will play tug-of-war with twigs, or crows will gang up to haze a greatly outnumbered cat. A crow may swing upside down on a branch, monkey style; or play drop-the-stick—flying down fast to catch it. One researcher saw a crow invent a log-rolling game in which it balanced on a plastic cup and rolled it down a hill. Then a sibling watching these antics followed suit. A neighbor of mine was surprised one afternoon to find crows, perched on the frame of her skylight, dropping pebbles onto the glass and watching them skitter.

Other animals are equally playful. Here is Wendell Berry describing a bird at play:

> I sat one summer evening and watched a great blue heron
> make his descent from the top of the hill into the valley. He
> came down at a measured deliberate pace, stately as always,

like a dignitary going down a stair. And then, at a point I judged to be midway over the river, without at all varying his wingbeat he did a backward turn in the air, a loop-the-loop. It could only have been a gesture of pure exuberance, of joy—a speaking of his sense of the evening, the day's fulfillment, his descent homeward. He made just that one slow turn, and then flew on out of sight in the direction of the slew farther down in the bottom. The movement was incredibly beautiful, at once exultant and stately, a benediction on the evening and on the river and on me. It seemed so perfectly to confirm the presence of a free nonhuman joy in the world.

For humans, play is a refuge from ordinary life, a sanctuary of the mind, where one is exempt from life's customs, methods, and decrees. Play always has a sacred place—some version of a playground—in which it happens. The hallowed ground is usually outlined, so that it's clearly set off from the rest of reality. This place may be a classroom, a sports stadium, a stage, a courtroom, a coral reef, a workbench in a garage, a church or temple, a field where people clasp hands in a circle under the new moon. Play has a time limit, which may be an intense but fleeting moment, the flexible innings of a baseball game, or the exact span of a psychotherapy session. Sometimes the time limit is prearranged; at other times it's only recognizable in retrospect. The world of play favors exuberance, license, abandon. Shenanigans are allowed, strategies can be tried, selves can be revised. In the self-enclosed world of play, there is no hunger. It is its own goal, which it reaches in a richly satisfying way. Play has its own etiquette, rituals and ceremonies, its own absolute rules. As Johan Huizinga notes in *Homo Ludens,* a classic study of play and culture, play "creates order, *is* order. Into an imperfect world and into the confusion of life it brings a temporary, limited perfection. The least deviation from it spoils the game." These are the basic rules of all forms of play. But play also has its own distinctive psychology.

Above all, play requires freedom. One chooses to play. Play's rules may be enforced, but play is not like life's other dramas. It happens outside ordinary life, and it requires freedom. Even animals that play instinctively do so because they enjoy play, choose to play when the mood strikes them, or they are invited to by other animals. But freedom alone doesn't ensure a playful result; people often choose the work they do, and not everyone is lucky enough to regard their work as play. Players like to invent substitute worlds, more advantageous outcomes of events, supplemental versions of reality, other selves. Make-believe is at the heart of play, and also at the heart of much of what passes for work. Let's make-believe we can shoot a rocket to the moon.

Most forms of play involve competition, against oneself or others, and test one's skills, cunning, or courage. One might even argue that all play is a contest of one sort or another. The adversary may be a mountain, a chess-playing computer, or an incarnation of evil. To play is to risk: to risk is to play. The word *fight* derives from the word *play*. Medieval tournaments were ritualized battles that followed strict rules. So are wrestling, boxing, and fencing matches. Ceremonial violence—at a sacred place, in which special clothes are worn, time limits must be obeyed, rules are followed, rituals are performed, the action is alarmingly tense, and the outcome is unknown—is elemental to play. Festive dancing may seem peaceful by comparison, and indeed in Anglo-Saxon, *play* was *plega,* which meant singing or dancing gestures, clapping, quick movements.

But when we peer even farther back into its origins, we discover that play's original meaning was quite different, something altogether more urgent and abstract. In Indo-European, *plegan* meant to risk, chance, expose oneself to hazard. A *pledge* was integral to the act of play, as was danger (cognate words are *peril* and *plight*). Play's original purpose was to make a pledge to someone or something by risking one's life. Who or what might that someone or something be? Possibilities abound, including a relative, a tribal leader, a god, or a moral trait such as honor or courage. At its heart, *plegan* reverberated with ethical or religious values. It also contained the idea of being tightly fastened or engaged. Soon *plegan* became associated with performing a sacred act or administering justice, and it often appeared in ceremonies. In a later chapter, I'll talk about the importance of those ceremonies.

However, not all ethical play requires risk and hazard. For example, an elementary school teacher I know teaches ethics through community service, inspiring children to have fun while doing good works. One overcast day in late October, she brought a hundred children and their parents to plant bulbs at the local hospice. They had learned earlier about what a hospice is, and discussed how much the flowers would mean to its residents. These would probably be the last flowers they saw. So the children understood the value of what they were doing, as they playfully ripped out hundreds of frost-killed cosmos and other annuals, dug 2,000 holes, raked dirt, planted glossy bulbs, chased the occasional shrew. Children and dirt, what could be better? In that bulb-planting project, teacher and students captured the gentler side of *plegan*. Organizations like Habitat for Humanity, where bighearted people volunteer to build homes for others—while enjoying the outdoors, hard work, and socializing—do the same.

By far the most common use of play words, in many languages, is the erotic. The Sanskrit word for copulation is *kridaratnam*, which translates as "the jewel of games." In German, a *Spielkind* (literally a "play child") is a baby born out of wedlock. In English, we make a play for, play up to, indulge in love play. Our word *lechery* evolved from *leik*, a root word for play. Among native Americans of the Blackfoot tribe, the word *koani* could be applied either to child's play or to unlawful sex. Words for play mainly gave rise to words used in love play, battle, or religious rites (*feast* and *festival* also trace their etymology to play). What do these activities have in common? They all require daring, risk, concentration, the ability to live with uncertainty, a willingness to follow the rules of the game, and a desire for transcendence. They share the spirit of sacred play, where the child and the poet are at home with the savage.

The savage is what we sometimes long to be—living by cunning and raw emotion, attuned to nature, senses alert, eluding danger, thrilled by challenge. "One thinks of Tolstoy among the Cossacks," Peter Marin writes in *Coevolution Quarterly,* "learning from the raw power of a life stripped clean of possessions and exposed to the rock-hard facts of the world. There was an austerity to their existence so pure that it became for him a kind of sensuality, and no doubt later in his life, when he wanted to strip himself morally to the bone, there was a similar element involved. There is a connection between moral power and the sense of exposure to the mortal elements."

Facing trials and winning is essential, especially if one is pitting the forces of good against the forces of evil. At such high-stakes gambling, luck is an important ingredient, of course; in many myths, gods wager with human life. In the Sanskrit *Mahabharata,* for example, we find men, who represent the seasons, deciding the world's weather and crop yield by rolling gold and silver dice. But, aside from luck or the favor of the gods, the player succeeds by his or her own talents. It's astonishing really, the extremes people have gone to in search of praise—for reassurance that they're accomplished, excellent beings who are valued. A Freudian has rich ground here, as does an evolutionary psychologist. What fuels a need to be publicly celebrated and declared good? Suppose the drive is ravenous, involving nations? Because prestige is an unstable element, warriors must constantly prove their merit, in relentless deeds of valor, and it doesn't

matter much these days if the battleground is an office or a boxing ring. A day passing without glory, however small, is cause
for anxiety. Ranks may shuffle, face may be lost, resources may
wane, potential mates may recede. Even apparently altruistic
acts may in truth be deeply concerned with merit and glory.
When a pilot recently flew his crippled jet into a mountain,
killing himself rather than risking many lives in a heavily popu-
lated area where he might have lucked out landing on a highway, people exclaimed "How selfless of him!" But one of his
motives, undoubtedly, was to act honorably; he couldn't live
with himself as a man who caused the deaths of many civilians.
We may call someone who sacrifices his life for another an altru-
ist, but his real motives may be less selfless than we imagine; they
may be profoundly concerned with valor and a coherent sense
of self.

Physical strength has traditionally been one test of nobility.
Also courage or great wealth. In twelfth-century Florence, the
elite competed by constructing a forest of towers, each more
spectacular than the next. Ostensibly created for defense, these
artful structures became known as "swagger towers." But in the
past, and in many cultures, contests usually included tests of
knowledge and wit. Ancient heroes were given sacred riddles to
solve, and a wrong answer meant death. Warriors battled one another with insults and boasts, as American street kids do today.
China even held a "courtesy match," in which rivals fought by
zealously out-politing each other. He whose manners were the
most overwhelmingly polite won. In courtrooms, armies also
battle with words. As became clear to multitudes of television
viewers during the O. J. Simpson murder trial, winning a court
case has little to do with right and wrong, but with how well
one's lawyers control the game. All such rivalries involve the idea
of trial, of publicly testing one's skill, nerve, or gifts. All this happens on the field of play. Huizinga argues that

[t]he rules of warfare, the conventions of noble living, were built up on play-patterns. We have to conclude, therefore, that civilization is, in its early phases, played. It does not come from play like a babe detaching itself from the womb: it arises *in* and *as* play, and never leaves it. . . . Fair play is nothing less than good faith expressed in play terms. Hence the cheat or the spoil-sport shatters civilization itself.

I think he's right. We don't pursue and punish lawbreakers just to keep them from repeating their crimes. They threaten us at a more basic level.

We usually think of play as self-indulgent and irresponsible. "Stop playing around, be serious!" someone might demand, as if the two clashed. Yet sports are the height of seriousness. In ancient Rome, "the games" included bloodthirsty crowds and gruesome deaths; and they could be whimsical: *let's see what happens if we pit a man against a bear or a crocodile.* Children can be extremely serious about play. Their games, though "fun," aren't always silly or filled with laughter.

Play is an activity enjoyed for its own sake. It is our brain's favorite way of learning and maneuvering. Because we think of play as the opposite of seriousness, we don't notice that it governs most of society—political games, in-law games, money games, love games, advertising games, to list only a few spheres where gamesmanship is rampant. Play may have different strengths, not all of them mystical and soul-stealing. But even in its least intoxicating forms, play feels satisfying, absorbing, and has rules and a life of its own, while offering rare challenges. It gives us the opportunity to perfect ourselves. It's organic to who and what we are, a process as instinctive as breathing. Much of human life unfolds as play.

This book explores an element of the human saga that has thrilled and fascinated me throughout my life: transcendent play. Not just how children play—rejoicing in the delights of silliness, perfecting their coordination, or rehearsing the rules of court-ship and society—but a special dimension of adult play. Something exquisitely human. Of course, adults often play in the same way and for the same reasons that children do; they act silly be-cause it's fun; they play to socialize, and that can include besting a rival or developing a friendship. But there is a deeper form of play, akin to rapture and ecstasy, that humans relish, even re-quire to feel whole.

A funny notion, feeling whole. If there is one thing a person knows for a fact, it is that he is trapped inside a suit of skin, that (unless he is a Siamese twin) he is not several, that if the armor of his body is pierced, he can bleed his innards away. He is a single self-contained entity. How peculiar not to feel whole. Plato's ex-planation is that each of us is, by design, only half a human, and therefore must search for a beloved to blend with to become whole. Feeling incomplete is an ancient delusion. Equally ancient is the attempt to feel whole by using drink, drugs, sex, prayer, mantras, sports, danger, and anything else one can think of to temporarily turn down the volume on the chatter in the brain. That absence of mental noise we find liberating, soothing, and ex-citing all at once.

Deep play is the ecstatic form of play. In its thrall, all the play elements are visible, but they're taken to intense and transcen-dent heights. Thus, deep play should really be classified by mood, not activity. It testifies to *how* something happens, not *what* hap-pens. Games don't guarantee deep play, but some activities are prone to it: art, religion, risk-taking, and some sports—especially those that take place in relatively remote, silent, and floaty envi-ronments, such as scuba diving, parachuting, hang gliding, moun-tain climbing.

Deep play always involves the sacred and holy, sometimes hidden in the most unlikely or humble places—amid towering shelves of rock in Nepal; crouched over print in a dimly lit room; slipping on AstroTurf; wearing a coconut-shell mask. We spend our lives in pursuit of moments that will allow these altered states to happen. The Australian Aborigines search for it on wilderness treks called walkabouts, during which young men of the tribe go alone into the dangerous outback to gain strength and wisdom. Buddhist lamas and Hindu sadhus travel, nearly naked, to pray atop glacial mountains in Tibet. People from many cultures have gone on soul journeys into the wilderness, where risk, hunger, pain, exhaustion, and sometimes self-torture might inspire visions. Young Masai men set off on a pilgrimage to Mount Kilimanjaro, the sacred center of their world, as part of the initiation rite known as Moranism. Native Americans have often used ritualized running to scale mental heights. The Hopis stage many such races every year, featuring paint, costumes, fasts, and prayer. The Crow Indians run to exhaustion to persuade the gods that they deserve good luck. The Zuni run twenty to forty miles while kicking a sacred stick. The official purpose of these ordeals may be religious, but the physiological goal is to impel the initiate into a higher state of consciousness that kindles visions and insights, in a locale where survival may depend on a combination of ingenuity and nerve.

Shamans and extreme athletes alike court deep play with a sensuous rigor bordering on mania. Creativity, psychotherapy, sensation-seeking—all are ideal playgrounds for deep play. Of late, I find many such moments while biking, but in the past I have found them riding horses, piloting light aircraft, scuba diving, studying animals in the wild, and exploring unfamiliar landscapes. Those moments have powered my dreams and yearnings, inspired most of my writing, and formed the basis of my spirituality. Over the next few pages, I'll quote briefly from several of my journals spanning roughly a decade. Although I wasn't aware of deep play at the time, I often lived it, unknowingly recorded its features, and chronicled many of its moods. This comes in handy now, as I explore the mental habitat of deep play, which has enriched my life for so long and powered the lives of so many others.

For about five years I traveled little and seemed to have few obvious moments of deep play. However, I was also in psychotherapy at the time and, in retrospect, that experience satisfied some of my needs. How can psychotherapy be experienced as deep play? All play happens in a special mental place, with time limits and rules, beyond everyday life. It contains uncertainty, illusion, an element of make-believe or fantasy, and allows one to take risks, or explore new roles. Psychoanalyst D. W. Winnicott, who spent a lifetime enthralled by the study of children, understood the value of engaging in the distinctive play of psychotherapy:

> Psychotherapy takes place in the overlap of two areas of playing, that of the patient and that of the therapist. Psychotherapy has to do with two people playing together . . . psychoanalysis has been developed as a highly specialized form of playing in the service of communication with oneself and others.

I was also a crisis counselor, a job that was full of intimate and tense dramas. So, in several ways, my life held an alternate reality outside the normal lull of routine, a high intensity and focus, perpetual risk, constant exposure to danger, fascination with another—all vital elements of deep play. British therapist Robin Skynner finds similarities between the dangerous exhilaration of his work and his experience flying Mosquito bombers during World War II. During counseling sessions, he would sometimes recognize the same "feeling of being absolutely attentive and completely *there*" that he used to feel at the moment when he was "going to drop a bomb. In both instances, I was dealing with something of an explosive nature. In therapy the aim is to defuse the bomb rather than try to escape from it or be blown up. It's very risky and exciting." I doubt that such high-wire intensity occurs in every session with every patient, but among the many rewards of his profession, therapy offers Skynner an opportunity for deep play.

The ancients wrote about and celebrated key elements of deep play, coining names for some of its moods. Because of them, for example, we know its "rapture" or its "ecstasy," and those words I too have used on the many occasions when I've felt deep play. Rapture and ecstasy are not themselves deep play, but they're central components of it.

Rapture means, literally, being "seized by force," as if one were a prey animal who is carried away. Caught in the talons of a transcendent rapture, one is gripped, elevated, and trapped at a fearsome height. To the ancient Greeks, this feeling often foretold malevolence and danger—other words that drink from the same rapturous source are *rapacious, rabid, ravenous, ravage, rape, usurp, surreptitious.* Birds of prey that plunge from the skies to gore their victims are known as *raptors.* Seized by a jagged and violent force, the enraptured are carried aloft to their ultimate doom.

Ecstasy also means to be gripped by passion, but from a slightly different perspective: rapture is vertical, ecstasy horizontal. Rapture is high-flying, ecstasy occurs on the ground. For some reason, the ancient Greeks were obsessed with the symbol of standing, and relied on that one image for countless ideas, feelings, and objects. As a result, a great many of our words today simply reflect where or how things stand: *stanchion, status, stare, staunch, steadfast, statute,* and *constant.* But there are also hundreds of unexpected ones, such as *stank* (standing water), *stallion* (standing in a stall), *star* (standing in the sky), *restaurant* (standing place for the wanderer), *prostate* (standing in front of the bladder), and so on. To the Greeks, ecstasy meant to stand outside onself. How is that possible? Through existential engineering. "Give me a place to stand," Archimedes proclaimed in the third century B.C., "and I will move the earth." Levered by ecstasy, one springs out of one's mind. Thrown free of one's normal self, a person stands in another place, on the limits of body, society, and reason, watching the known world dwindle in the *distance* (a spot standing far away). The euphoria of flying in dreams, or the longing to fly through the ocean with dolphins, fills us with rapture. Can one feel ecstasy and rapture at the same time? "The heart of standing is you cannot fly," William Empson muses in a poem about the simultaneous limits and grandeur of a love affair. These are two escape routes from the mundane, two paths to deep play, equally quenching, equally mystical, and subtly different. All roads may indeed lead to Rome, but one might be hilly, the other marshy.

In seventeenth-century France, the fashionably risqué sometimes bragged about an "ecstasy of delight" or an "ecstasy of rage"—passions wild as a seizure, with just a tincture of blasphemy to add a little soul-fearing frisson. But the word mainly referred to mystics and deeply religious people entranced to the point of subtraction from the world. I suppose it's a telling sign of our times that we now regard both rapture and ecstasy as pleasurable, desirable, even enviable states.

Whichever word you choose—rapture or ecstasy—each is fundamental to the notion of deep play. So is transcendence, risk, obsession, pleasure, distractedness, timelessness, and a sense of the holy or sacred. Over the years, some writers have illuminated important facets of the human condition that are related in one way or another to deep play. At the dawn of the twentieth century, Émile Durkheim wrote about "collective effervescence," a group form of deep play that occurs during ritualized events; and Victor Turner later wrote similarly about a feeling of "communitas," when the usual social roles are temporarily suspended. Freud wrote of the infant's craving for an "oceanic feeling," during which it seems to merge with the beloved or its environment. D. W. Winnicott wrote about play as a creative state of withdrawal from everyday life. D. E. Berlyne argued that organisms don't strive for perfect calm and quiet, but, on the contrary, need an "optimal" amount of stimulation to feel well. Mihalyi Csikszentmihalyi has written about "flow," a term commonly used by his research subjects to describe a mood of effortless enjoyment. Karl Groos and G. Murphy wrote about the special pleasure that comes from using one's body and senses to the fullest. Sartre, Heraclitus, Plato, and Nietzsche have emphasized the appeal of control and freedom in play. Dutch anthropologist Johan Huizinga wrote inspiringly about play and society. Abraham H. Maslow wrote of "peak experiences . . . of ecstasy, rapture, bliss, the greatest joy," transcendent states that also include "awe, mystery, complete perfection, humility, surrender, and worship." Healthy ("self-actualizing") people often experience such inherently rewarding moments as they discover their capabilities and limits.

The spirit of deep play is central to the life of each person, and also to society, inspiring the visual, musical, and verbal arts; exploration and discovery; war; law; and other elements of culture we've come to cherish (or dread). Swept up by the deepest states of play, one feels balanced, creative, focused. Deep play is a fascinating hallmark of being human; it reveals our need to seek a special brand of transcendence, with a passion that makes thrill-seeking explicable, creativity possible, and religion inevitable. Perhaps religion seems an unlikely example of playing, but if you look at religious rites and festivals, you'll see all the play elements, and also how deep that play can become. Religious rituals usually include dance, worship, music, and decoration. They swallow time. They are ecstatic, absorbing, rejuvenating. The word "prayer" derives from the Latin *precarius,* and contains the idea of uncertainty and risk. Will the entreaty be answered? Life or death may depend on the outcome. Because a system of sacrificial rites is essentially the same the world over, Huizinga concludes

> such customs must be rooted in a very fundamental, an ab-
> original layer of the human mind ... the concept of play
> merges quite naturally with that of holiness ... archaic ritual
> is thus sacred play, indispensable for the community, fecund
> of cosmic insight and social development but always play in
> the sense Plato gave to it—an action accomplishing itself
> outside and above the necessities and seriousness of everyday
> life. In this sphere of sacred play the child and the poet are at
> home with the savage.

From time to time, this book becomes a fantasia on a theme by Huizinga, in which I play with some of his ideas, amplify them, follow their shadows and nuances. However, I've borrowed the phrase *deep play* from Jeremy Bentham (1748–1832), the father of utilitarianism, who dismisses as "deep play" any activity in which "the stakes are so high that ... it is irrational for anyone to engage in it at all, since the marginal utility of what you stand to win is grossly outweighed by the disutility of what you stand to lose." This is true of so many human endeavors that one can scarcely read the newspaper without marveling at what someone some-where has decided she must do, come what may. Scratch the sur-face of an apparently low-key life, and you may find a passion for cross-country skiing that borders on frenzy, or a collection of stamps the owner pores over with monklike devotion as hours evaporate, because it contains the equivalent of holy relics.

Bentham despises deep play precisely for some of the reasons that I and others cherish it. For example, rock climber Mo Anthoine once confessed that a couple of times a year he had to *feed his rat,* as he put it, by which he meant that wonderful mad rodent inside him that demanded a challenge or a trip that would combine adventure, fun, wonder, risk, and ordeal. Although I'm not a rock climber, I know how the rat gnaws, and I agree there is nothing like deep play. Risk stimulates romance, and deep play thrives on a romance with life. Intense creativity is one form of deep play, whose origins psychologist Phyllis Greenacre helps illuminate. After years of clinical study of children, she concluded that often those destined to become artists were children who didn't have a reliable relationship with their caretakers. Instead, they developed (or made do with) "a love affair with the world." While in the Antarctic, I wrote in my journal:

> Tonight the moon is invisible, darkness itself has nearly vanished, and the known world which we map with families, routines, and newspapers, floats somewhere beyond the horizon. Traveling to a strange, new landscape is a kind of romance. You become intensely aware of the world where you are, but also oblivious to the rest of the world at the same time. Like love, travel makes you innocent again. The only news I've heard for days has been the news of nature. Tomorrow, when we drift through the iceberg gardens of Gerlache Strait, I will be working—that is, writing prose. My mind will become a cyclone of intense alertness, in which details present themselves slowly, thoroughly, one at a time. I don't know how to describe what happens to me when I'm out in "nature" and "working"—it's a kind of rapture—but it's happened often enough that I know to expect it.

I was already on the threshold of a great adventure, ready for the rapture I knew awaited me in the morning. I knew it would be a cyclone of intense alertness, a marginally frightening state in which I would exist entirely in the tense present and feel quintessentially alive.

That journal entry reports many of the elements of deep play. One enters into an alternate reality with its own rules, values, and expectations. One sheds much of one's culture, with its countless technical and moral demands, as one draws on a wholly new and sense-ravishing way of life. We think of "brainwashing" in the most negative terms, as a bizarre, powerfully effective ordeal that happens during wartime, when a prisoner is abducted and isolated. All contact with his past is severed, and he is forced to develop a different mental arcade, one exploitable by the enemy and including values opposite to those he previously cherished. However, there is another, positive form of that drama, in which one *chooses* to divest oneself of preconceptions, hand-me-down ideas, and shopworn opinions, *chooses* to wipe the mental slate clean, *chooses* to be naive and wholly open to the world, as one once was as a child. If cynicism is inevitable as one ages, so is the yearning for innocence. To children heaven is being an adult, and to adults heaven is being children again.

When lovers isolate themselves from others, desperate to be alone together, indeed when they decide to become "a couple," they escape to the sacred kingdom of their love affair, a private world with its own customs, dialect, values, and rules. Love is a voluntary mysticism. They become a cult of two. They often address each other in baby talk, using the same diminutives and endearments parents lavish on children. They tend to romp together, to become playmates. The lover is like a shaman who rises into steep ecstasy and thus is able to see into the heart and soul of the beloved. If one lover breaks up with the other, their secret world is shattered, its reality is disavowed, and in a sense the leaving partner becomes what children like to refer to as "a spoilsport," someone who ruins the game by rejecting its reality, essence, and appeal. Disavow the illusion and the game is over. Ignore a bully and he loses his power to frighten. Ignore a siren and she loses her power to enthrall. The word *illusion* literally means "in play." When the game of love is no longer in play, we say "the magic is gone," some of our best illusions have been shattered, and we return to the all-too-ordinary world.

This is not only true of lovers. People isolated in tense, dramatic situations of any kind—war, expeditions, initiation rituals, cruises, clubs—can dwell in a powerfully romantic and magical world set off from the rest of reality. Sometimes the players disguise themselves with masks, uniforms, or costumes. Sometimes they speak a private language. Sometimes they share holy secrets. Oscar Wilde said the essence of romance is uncertainty. And what could be more uncertain than danger? As many researchers have discovered, people fall in love far more readily when they're away from home, afraid of death, or both. Danger narrows and deepens your focus. So does love. So does prayer. As the world reduces to a small brilliant space, where every thought and move is vital to one's salvation, one's scattered energy suddenly has a center. Only then do all of our senses spring alert, and every sensation matters. At the same time, the rest of the world recedes. One is temporarily unshackled from life's chains—the family ones, the work ones, the ones we wear as self-imposed weights. In my pilot's journal in 1980, I wrote:

> It isn't that I find danger ennobling, or that I require cheap excitation to cure the dullness of routine; but I do like the moment central to danger and to some sports, when you become so thoroughly concerned with acting deftly, in order to be safe, that only reaction is possible, not analysis. You shed the centuries and feel creatural. Of course, you do have to scan, assess, and make constant minute decisions. But there is nothing like *thinking* in the usual, methodical way. What takes

its place is more akin to an informed instinct. For a pensive person, to be fully alert but free of thought is a form of ecstasy . . . there is also a state when perception doesn't work, consciousness vanishes like the gorgeous fever it is, and you feel free of all mind-body constraints, suddenly so free of them you don't perceive yourself as being free, but vigilant, a seeing eye without judgment, history, or emotion. It's that shudder out of time, the central moment in so many sports, that one often feels, and perhaps becomes addicted to, while doing something dangerous.

In later years, on expeditions to extraordinary landscapes, I discovered it is possible to enter the mansions of nature so profoundly that time vibrates in a new way. Moments may sprawl for hours or race by in a panic, split into separate photographic stills presenting themselves one by one, or pile up, or whirl breathlessly like a beautiful tornado. In deep play, one's sense of time no longer originates within oneself. This shift in time often happens to people who work with wild animals, especially if they set out on expeditions to unknown lands.

On one such trip, to a remote Japanese island to find the last surviving short-tailed albatrosses, I fell on a cliff and broke three ribs. After that, life became terrifyingly dangerous. At twilight, when like monks we finished our silent beholding, we gathered up our knapsacks and considered the ascent. Hampered by a tight straitjacket of pain, I could not move the left side of my body. Yet somehow we had to climb back up the 400-foot cliff, hike across a volcano to the small, abandoned garrison that was our base camp, and then try to find a way off the island for medical help.

"A great day, despite everything," I told my companions, and meant it. "Who would drink from a cup when they can drink from the source?"

That drama highlights another facet of deep play. We want to muscle into life and feel its real power and sweep. We want to drink from the source. In rare moments of deep play, we can lay aside our sense of self, shed time's continuum, ignore pain, and sit quietly in the absolute present, watching the world's ordinary miracles. No mind or heart hobbles. No analyzing or explaining. No questing for logic. No promises. No goals. No relationships. No worry. One is completely open to whatever drama may unfold. With innocent surprise, one regards life's spectacles and underpinnings. All one feels is affectionate curiosity for the whole bustling enterprise of creation. It doesn't matter what prompts the feeling— watching albatrosses court or following the sky-blown oasis of a tumultuous sunset. When it happens we experience a sense of revelation and gratitude. Nothing need be thought or said. There is a way of beholding that is a form of prayer.

Deep time isn't a realm into which one accidentally tumbles. Dozens of choices may lead up to it, *normal* time may surround it. There is usually a boundary or door at the edge of deep time. I think of such edges as "littoral moments" because they are like the thin skirtings of sand along seashores that connect the solid land to the fluency of waves. There are moments on the brink, when you can give yourself to a lover, or not; give in to self-doubt, uncertainty, and admonishment, or not; dive into a different culture, or not; set sail for the unknown, or not; walk out onto a stage, or not. A moment only a few seconds long, when your future hangs in the balance, poised above a chasm. It is a crossroads. Resist then, and there is no returning to the known world. If you turn back, there is only what might have been. Above that invisible crossroads are inscribed the words: *Give up your will, all who travel here.*

Giving up my will, self, uniqueness—happily, with a saint's devotion—has its own special appeal. As does lending my sensibility to someone else so that he or she may speak through it, sharing their vision in a coherent language. I suppose I try to be a translator of sorts, striving to translate emotion and vision into words, to express the life force of animals and landscapes, to give them voice. I pore over the lustrous details of nature and human nature. How different is this from a monk devoting his life to an illuminated manuscript?

What is the difference between simple play and deep play? Simple play can take many forms and have many purposes, but it goes only so far. When it starts focusing one's life and offering ecstatic moments, it becomes deep play. Evolution fiddling with one phenomenon—such as color or flight—is an example of play at its most basic, where bare bones are revealed. Even without mind, it is still ingeniously varied and full of risk. When animals rehearse techniques they'll need as adults, or gambol about to keep their wits and muscles keen, another form of play becomes visible. But this is not deep play. Neither is something done because of obligation or threat. Concentrating for long hours in a demanding job is not deep play. Jogging because you know it's good for you is not deep play. Playing a sport hard because a lot of money and/or reputation is riding on your performance is not deep play. Repeating prayers or singing hymns that have grown stale is not deep play. Deep play is not always positive and uplifting. Gang members sometimes describe their exploits as a perverse rapture. However, in deep play's altered mental state one most often finds clarity, revelation, acceptance of self, and other life-affirming feelings.

There are times during deep play when one feels invincible, immortal, an ideal version of oneself. "One stands on the threshold of miracles," basketball player Patsy Neal writes about peak experiences during a game. "The power of the moment adds up to a certain amount of religion in the performance. Call it a state of grace, or an act of faith . . . or an act of God. . . . The individual becomes swept up in the action around her—she almost floats through the performance, drawing on forces she has never previously been aware of. In those precious moments of pure ecstasy," Neal continues, one "runs and jumps and *lives* through the pure play process, which is composed of joy and pleasure and exuberance and laughter; even the pain seems completely tolerable in these few precious and rare moments of *being,* and of knowing that one is just that . . . a oneness and a wholeness." Substitute gospel singing or painting for playing basketball in Neal's description, and it would be equally true.

Time and again, risk-seekers report a combination of heightened awareness and omnipotence. In *Bone Games,* climber Rob Schultheis recalls how he felt descending a mountain after a harrowing near-death fall: "The person I became on Neva was the best possible version of myself, the person I *should have been* throughout my life. No regrets, no hesitation; there were no false moves left in me. I really believe I could have hit a mosquito in the eye with a pine needle at thirty paces; I couldn't miss because there was no such thing as a miss." Charles Lindbergh wrote of seeing ghost companions who helped him navigate on his famous 1926 solo flight, and gave him "messages of importance unattainable in ordinary life." Swiss geologist Albert von St. Gallen Heim, who interviewed survivors of climbing falls for his 1892 monograph *Remarks on Fatal Falls,* found that they had had similar experiences:

> . . . there was no anxiety, no trace of despair, no pain . . . mental activity became enormous, rising to a hundredfold velocity or intensity. The relationship of events and their probable outcomes were overviewed with objective clarity. The individual acted with lightning quickness.

Schulteis credits "stress-triggered ecstasy" for transcendent experiences, the same rush produced by vision quests and sought by shamans. Moses climbed Mount Sinai to speak with God, Mohammed climbed Mount Hira, Buddha experienced years of deprivation in the lowlands. Pain, exhaustion, hunger, stress, isolation, risk—all are frequently used by shamans, extreme athletes, saints, and others to flog the body into enlightened states.

The sacred playground may be as grand as the Grand Canyon, as fluid as the ocean where dolphins swim, as crowded as a jazz club, or even as invisible as a cyberchurch on the Internet. Deep play's extreme versions may include death-defying feats, during which one tends to feel remarkably tranquil. "You feel a calmness through your body," motorcycle racer Malcolm Smith reports, "even though you know intellectually that you're right on the brink of disaster." Challenge, discovery, exploration, novelty, pushing one's limits, losing one's self in the activity— elements of deep play—occur for Smith when he races motorcycles. However, not all people who ride motorcycles undergo the same enthusiasm. For some, racing is work; for others it is play; but for Smith, it is deep play.

This book is not a conclusion but an exploration. It invites you to look closely at the human saga, and consider how much of it revolves around play. Basic play, elaborate play, crude play, sophisticated play, violent play, casual play. Most animals play. Evolution itself plays with lifeforms. Whole cultures play with customs, ideas, belief systems, and fashions. But it's a special caliber of play—deep—that leads to transcendence, creativity, and a need for the sacred. Indeed, it's our passion for deep play that makes us the puzzling and at times resplendent beings we are. By a happy coincidence, this book is itself an example of its theme. The writing of it includes many moments of play, some purer and more transcendent than others. I've allowed those moments to hover a bit, as they do in life, because that shudder out of time is how deep play always begins.

CHAPTER TWO

At-One-Ment

(Purification Through Deep Play)

So then, let Thy fear, O Yahweh our God, come over all Thy creatures, and reverent dread of Thee upon all that Thou hast made, that all Thy creatures may fear Thee and every being bow before Thee and that they may all become bonded together to do Thy will with all their heart, even as we know, O Yahweh our God, that Thine is the lordship, that might is in Thy left hand and power in Thy right hand and Thy name exalted above all that Thou hast created.

—Jewish prayer

The bicycle, the bicycle surely, should always be the vehicle of novelists and poets. . . . as [the poet] passes from windy hill-top to green creeks and grazings sometimes the bicycle sets him free. He sees it all afresh; nothing, nothing has ever been written yet: the entire white paper of the world is clean for his special portrait of all hunger, all joy, and all vexation.

—Christopher Morley, *The Romany Stain* (1926)

Yom Kippur, the Jewish Day of Atonement. The liturgy includes
prayers that tremble with the "reverent dread" of early religions.
It is a day dedicated to regret, apology, and atonement, which is itself a fascinating human obsession. Do other animals feel debased
by acting badly? As any dog owner will tell you, some animals do
know when they've done something forbidden. But our powerful
frenzy of self-disgust when we transgress moral codes or commit
evil is uniquely human. Furthermore, as Rudolf Otto reminds us
in his classic study, *The Idea of the Holy,* no religion expresses our innate need for atonement as eloquently as Christianity, which has
raised it to a powerful and elaborate art form. He traces the mental
course that begins with feelings of guilt about doing something
bad to the need for ceremonial purification:

The evil of the action *weighs upon us* and deprives us of our self-respect. We *accuse* ourselves and *remorse* sets in. But alongside this self-depreciation stands a second one. . . . The same perverse action that before weighed upon us now *pollutes* us; we do not accuse ourselves, we are defiled in our own eyes. And the characteristic form of emotional reaction is no longer remorse but *loathing*. The man feels a need, to express which he has recourse to images of *washing* and cleansing . . . the need for atonement.

Are we to atone only for sins of commission, or for sins of omission, too? And how deep should that atonement run? For example, the sun set today without my celebrating it, without trying to capture it in a net of words. Out of laziness, distractedness, or selfishness, I did other things instead. I played in the garden. I made a map of one flower bed, with plastic overlays on which I drew each season's additional plants. Then I slowly laid one see-through sheet on top of another, picturing the flowers that would bloom and vanish with the changing seasons, and others that would bloom for months on end. I loved picturing purple pea pods climbing two white trellises. But suppose somewhere there are people who need the tonic of the sunset? Maybe not fifty or even ten of them. Suppose there is only one, say a young man who is trapped in a tough home life where he doesn't have a nourishing relationship with any caregiver. Suppose, to use Phyllis Greenacre's insights, he is nonetheless surviving with grace by developing a love affair with the world, a sense of admiration and awe that will save him?

Why do risk-takers and extreme athletes alike speak so often of *purification* as the desired outcome of their deep-play ordeal? Why do they feel in need of *cleansing*? For what do they require death-defying feats of atonement? That cleansing the mind and body may offer relief from the strain of constant awareness and perception, and therefore *feels* good, doesn't explain the extremes certain people choose for that cleansing, or the relentlessness of their compulsion. Christianity's idea of original sin has been hugely successful because it taps into a feeling most humans experience: a sense of free-floating guilt, a need for self-improvement, a belief that there is a best version of oneself one can become, someone more lovable, someone of higher status. We can imagine states of perfection we cannot achieve. Such are the phantoms of consciousness. But, given that innate tendency, some people struggle more than others, some feel a greater need to become a person they can live with, to establish harmony in the self. I believe that feeling is forged in the brazier of relationships, probably early ones. The symbolism is suspicious. Babies are "baptized" to cleanse their soiled spirit. How soiled can it be? All mammalian mothers clean their infants so that they'll thrive; most lick them clean. For adults, such acts return them emotionally to the safety and absolute love of infancy. Indeed, those are the words people use: being reborn. How does one arrive at that literally impossible place? Magically, symbolically, by extreme acts that prove one is deserving, acts so risky, focused, or exhausting they seem to erase all one has been, all one has thought, all failures and yearnings, all expectations of oneself. One can also grovel and perform clear acts of contrition and apology.

When one *atones,* the guilt may be washed away, the slate wiped clean. Of course, life being the moral sty it is, one soon becomes redefiled and again needs to atone. A Freudian might say that, deprived of adequate parenting, some internalize the harsh tribunal of their parents and spend their lives trying to gain the impossible love of phantoms. Unclear about their motives, they feel as if they have reparations to pay for the war crimes of their youth—but the details are foggy. Atonement literally meant reestablishing a lost bond with a god or gods, an at-one-ment with a higher force and judge, in order once more to be protected, fed, and favored. Or, to put it another way, some people stage their own personal initiation rites before parent-gods, the cosmos, or an imaginary jury of peers. They are never alone on their mountain or ice yacht, but accompanied by hard-to-impress ghosts. I suppose it's made worse by the strange little truth that, when the chips are down, we tend to compare our insides to other people's outsides, and thus end up feeling like con men and fakes. Were it possible, we would start over again, pure as a newborn, in the hope of following a more sacred path. If that's not possible, and it never is, then the next-best step is to try to strip down to acquired innocence, wash away our selfish hungers and all the wicked humors of the world. Benjamin DeMott, in a study of parachute jumpers, explains that for the jumper "it amounts to a ritual of divestiture—a means of stripping off layers of institutional lies and myths that encrust the Individual.... Man diving is man alive; the ecstasy is that of non-connection—the exhilaration of sinking the world to nothingness, or at least to stillness, and thereby creating the self as All." When one enters the realm of deep play, the sacred playground where only the present moment matters, one's history and future vanish. One doesn't remember one's past, needs, expectations, worries, real or imaginary sins. The deep-play world is fresh, wholly absorbing, and full of its own unique wisdom and demands. Being able to temporarily step outside of normal life—while keeping one's senses alert—is indeed like being reborn. To erase all memories and yearnings—to be vigorously alive without self-awareness—can provide a brief return to innocence. "No human being is innocent," poet W. H. Auden observes, "but there is a class of innocent actions called games."

Such are my thoughts as I bike down a hot country road where a mirage of water waits twenty yards ahead but always out of reach.

Finally I turn toward the cooler sanctuary of a woods. I love the
dream state of biking and its many circles: the wheels within
wheels, the circular motion of the legs, the circling of the seasons,
the circular journeys that usually end back where they began
but with renewed zest and added experience. A low growl of
macadam quickly changes to dirt quiet and the occasional chatter of twigs and leaves. A biting sun gives way to the dappled light
of the forest, and I become aware of my back curved over the
yellow bike frame, flexing with the bike; and of my feet pushing
gently like pistons but also floating. The sensation of floating,
which figures in our dreams, is often experienced by mystics and
meditators, and also frequently reported by runners, dancers,
climbers, joggers.

"The flesh becomes light and transparent," Isadora Duncan
writes in *The Art of Dance,* "a luminous moving cloud . . . the whole
of its divinity." Margherita Duncan, Isadora's sister-in-law, described the rapture of watching Isadora dance: "When she danced
the *Blue Danube,* her simple waltzing forward and back, like the
oncoming and receding waves on the shore, had such an ecstasy
of rhythm that audiences became frenzied with the contagion of
it, and could not contain themselves, but rose from their seats,
cheering, applauding, laughing and crying. . . . We felt as if we
had received the blessing of God." Of course, dance-induced ecstasy has a long religious tradition, most famously associated with
the whirling dervishes. "In the midst of this abandonment of
self, or rather religious delirium," John Porter Brown writes in
Darvishes, "they make use of red-hot irons. . . . These fanatics,
transported by frenzy, seize upon these irons, gloat upon them,
bite them, hold them between their teeth, and end by cooling
them in their mouths."

That's a bit more fire and float than I need, so I'm happy to
leave the red-hot irons to dervishes. While cycling, I tend to
commune with nature, feel life's elements, and repeat a simple

mantra of sensations that I experience separately: blue sky, white clouds, green trees, apple scent, bright sun, warm breeze. Not all bike rides begin and end in a meditation on the senses. But I try at least to keep worries, sorrows, and mind theaters to a minimum, and open myself up to the textures and processes of life. If I focus only on sensations, the world unfolds in a hundred fascinating directions.

Sometimes I become aware of my grip on the handlebars. What a marvel of design is the human hand. The hand is action, it digs roads and builds cities, it throws spears and diapers babies. And even a small drama like pushing a button can change the course of nations. Nerves in our hands send messages about touch, pressure, heat, cold, and pain up 17,000 fibers to the brain. Without that intricate feel for life there would be no artists to make sensory and emotional maps of the world. We've become voluptuaries of touch. We feel our way through life from birth to death. After all, touch is what leads us outside ourselves. Touch is what gives us our grasp on life. But most of all it allows us to rejoice in one another, our friends and loved ones, our neighbors and families. And perhaps that is the most touching thought of all. Because touch makes the world tantalizing and rich, it's part of the merchandise being sold in catalogues and chic stores: massaging chairs, mattresses, and implements. Without touch we would live in a sensory desert. As our most erotic sense, it's also subject to many taboos. If a couple isn't married, their caresses would be illegal under the laws of many nations. Touch reminds us of that time when Mother cradled us, and we felt safe, adored, and perfectly lovable. As adults, we still crave those affectionate touches.

A low-flying bluejay steals my attention. Sapsucker Woods is incredibly beautiful in this season. Shriveled ferns have turned shades of orange-brown. Shallow water under the raised walkways makes a single black smear, with golden pine needles lying on a brilliant collage. The bike wheels sound like the *shushing* of children dragging their shoes through fallen leaves. A mirror world glows in the pond's shining ebony. Focus on the world inside the mirror, the rippling chiaroscuro, and you can slide down into it. Leaves float on top like gondolas, but a hidden reality seems to vibrate below. The sky in that kingdom is deeper, more brooding, darker than the actual sky above Sapsucker Woods. It's limitless as the real sky is limitless, but a shadow reality rules the water world: all its elements are real, all its apparitions are real; yet it is not real. In this three-dimensional jigsaw puzzle, the fact that images are upside down is almost incidental.

As fish and insects touch the surface, they distort the picture. A gentle sunlight lies like tufts of cotton wool in the clumped grasses. The air has a razor clarity to it, a brilliance and sharpness that highlights a dragonfly weaving over the pond—here and there pausing, as if displayed inside a glass paperweight. When a light breeze shakes the surface of the water, colors ripple over tree trunks perfectly portrayed all the way down to the encrustations of fungi and peeling of bark. Surely one could peer underneath the islands of matted leaves and see to the distant shore. About twenty half-decayed logs lie like alligators, snout under leaves, front legs in the pond, trunk on the land.

Leaving the pond's upside-down planetarium, I ride in the opposite direction, where everything suddenly looks new. When deep play grows stale, one can simply change the perspective. How to do that even more? Well, one way might be to leave my bike home and return on horseback, jogging along, head at branch level, changing all the sounds, relaxing, being transported, viewing the forest from a moving perch. I've always loved horses. Rhythmic, voluptuous, full of snort and lather, horses are fun to ride, but they are also fun to think. Play with the idea of horses. Maybe they were vital to all we have become. Maybe we're indebted to them for much of our humanity. Maybe the airplane and electronics revolutions pale by comparison with the equine one.

As we flinch from the zealous assaults of technology, which have turned daily life into an obstacle course of billboards, and upped the ante so high that kindergarten children now use word processors, it's easy to forget that feeling overwhelmed is a relative state. Someone riffling through human history might not find our computer age a revolutionary pinnacle; they might choose something like the domestication of the horse, which vastly altered the culture, character, language, mobility, and even the look of human beings. With bridled horses, we galloped across continents and returned with a treasury of words, seeds, and in-laws.

James Watt, an eighteenth-century engineer, decided that if he wished people to understand the power of his new invention—the steam engine—he would need to compare it to a team of horses. He measured how much weight a single brewery horse could pull, and concluded that, in one minute, one horse could move 33,000 pounds one foot. We still calibrate machinery in horsepower and if that seems archaic it also feels viscerally right, because horses have amplified the destiny of everyone on earth. Horses have made civilization possible.

Long after dogs, sheep, and cattle became familiars, around the third millennium B.C., humans first began to domesticate horses, to rope and bridle them for work, and then to think of them as possible extensions of the human body. It must have taken blood-and-thunder courage for the first person to leap onto the back of a wild, biting, bucking, limb-flailing horse, but that act of daring led to a world filled with such ordinary miracles as airplane flight.

Horses changed our lives irreversibly. People no longer conducted romances as they did before horses—suddenly they could court someone from across the river, or in a different valley. "Courting distance" was twelve miles—how far a rider could comfortably ride, spend a little time visiting, and return home, all in one day. The relationship of married children and parents changed; they could visit often; good-bye was not forever; there was no need to abandon them if they married someone from a far-flung town. People no longer fought wars only with neighbors. Mounted attacks were to be feared, and it made sense to condense dwellings into a small area for mutual defense. Riders could carry silk, spices, and other trade goods to far lands. Families could arrange marriages over greater distances, even with people in other countries, and so the gene pool began to change. Riders sowed the seeds of language and culture throughout the world. In time, the horse carried such trends as "romantic love" from the Middle East through Spain and into southern France. The horse altered the way people earned their livings, how they educated their young, where they vacationed, how they thought of news, what sports they played, how they raised crops, where they worshiped, how they conducted government, and whether or not they could rescue one another in the event of catastrophes. The horse revamped the limits of our personal freedom, and enriched what we mean by a pilgrimage. Most of all, it enhanced how we picture the human body, that personal space in which we live, making it elastic and swift. If one wished, one could ride to town for a quick chore or a social gathering. Until very recently, horses completely dominated one's business and leisure hours. It was inconceivable to imagine a world without horses being used for transport, portage, sports, and war.

For most of human history, horses were the ultimate, most advanced form of transportation, and that made them seem miraculous as spaceships. When Cortés landed in the New World, with sixteen of his men on horseback, the wonderstruck Aztecs thought they were looking at manifold gods. In a sense, they were right. The human body, once cramped and slow, had attached itself to a swift, powerful horse. It became a biological mosaic, a thinking fury that could gallop through forests, swamps, and deserts. This symbiosis felt right then, in some deep, organic way, and it has felt right ever since, even majestic. Humans are a running species. Graceful and fast, muscular and compact, we identify with the fugitive spirit of a horse. The human "race" longs to be *off like a shot, burn up the road, get the lead out, make tracks, hightail it, vamoose,* or *skedaddle.* We who use the word "run" to describe the success of nearly everything, even apply the word to clocks, which seems a fair choice, since running horses revolutionized our sense of time. When you can sprint across the earth at twenty miles an hour, how can you endure the tardiness of a shopkeeper? If a relay of riders can cross a frontier in one day, how can you possibly wait longer than that for an important message to arrive?

Horses have always tantalized a wild and ancient part of us. But for women the relationship goes even deeper, to the core of their psychology, self-definition, and sexuality. Adolescent girls tend to obsess about horses, and, unbeknownst to them, it's an idolatry with an ancient past. Early human history is drenched with horse worship. Irish kings used to worship their goddess, Epona, the White Mare. Her chalk effigy, nearly 400 feet long, still surveys a hillside in Berkshire, England. This religion, based on horse worship, wasn't just a small cult limited to Britain; it thrived in Scandinavia, Europe, Greece, and India. Indeed, its holy days were still being celebrated, along with Christian ones, in Europe as late as the sixteenth century. The animal that appears most often in the Lascaux cave is the horse, and there are great magical herds of them, painted in perspective, and with seasonal and behavioral details lovingly observed. Today horses fire our imaginations just as surely as they did then. "The proverb is the horse of conversation," the Dahomeans of West Africa say proverbially. Domesticating horses has greatly altered our lives, but it hasn't diluted our sense of mysticism and awe. Atop Everest, holy flags flutter, bearing written prayers and images of winged horses. The flags, left by Sherpas on the ledge of the world, invoke their deities with words, and the horses are sacred spirits who will speed the prayers to heaven. *Lung ta* is what the Sherpas call the small, powerful pennants. For convenience, and because our world is less animistic than theirs, we translate this as "prayer flag," but no doubt Sherpas hear galloping hooves in the rhythmic flapping. To them, *lung ta* means "wind horse."

There was a time when riding a horse was like riding a whirlwind, and galloping across the tundra atop a half ton of snorting, whinnying, barely controlled panic was deep play enough. The only problem is that when peak experiences are repeated they often lose their intensity. Familiarity reduces the thrill. *Oh, that again,* the mind says with a yawn, *another gallop, another balloon crossing, another summit.* Mastery may be what we strive for, but once we achieve it we lose the novelty, innocence, tension, the striving for accomplishment, and all the other attributes of a satisfying challenge that's only a hairbreadth more doable than it isn't. We lose enthusiasm, our possession by the gods. The same drug doesn't springboard us to the same heights. So we increase the dose, raise the stakes, choose a more dangerous climb (or the same one, but solo or without oxygen), attempt an even more devilish piano sonata.

The spirit of deep play is spontaneity, discovery, and being open to new challenges. As a result, it allows one to happily develop new skills, test one's limits, stretch them, and then maybe refine the skills and redefine the limits. What is its biological purpose? Not basic survival. It carries one across fear and uncertainty toward the slippery edges of possibility, where one must use oneself fully and stretch human limits to achieve the remarkable. It encourages discovery and growth. At first that feels thrillingly satisfying, but tedium sets in and we're soon eager for more, for something requiring greater skills, greater risk, newer challenges. One can see how important this trait might be in our own evolution. A new scheme, thrilling at first, rapidly becomes ordinary, and finally dull. Craving more moments of deep play, we set bigger challenges, develop new skills, take greater chances, canvass worlds.

Humans love playing with other animals, and sometimes this leads to a purity of exchange almost magical in its intensity, deep play at its best. For instance, I once heard about a friendly group of spotted dolphins that are drawn to music played underwater and

readily swim with divers in the warm currents of the Bahamas. Research teams visit yearly to chronicle their history and habits. Villagers in the sea, the dolphins form a community that changes as couples mate, young are born, the aged die, and new alliances are forged. There is nothing like the indelible thrill of meeting a wild animal on its own terms in its own element, so I decided to join a week-long trip. One morning I flew to Grand Bahama, took a cab to the West End, and boarded a two-masted schooner along with eight other researchers. We were hoping to encounter spotted dolphins often enough during the week at sea to be able to identify and catalogue individuals.

At six-thirty the following morning, we left the West End behind and cruised toward the Little Bahama Bank, a shallow area that spotted dolphins seem to prefer. After a few minutes, we hoisted the mainsail, from which two rows of short ties hung like fringe. Then we sat on benches or low deck chairs, finding shade under a large blue canopy stretched over the center of the boat and attached by a web of ropes over the boom. The ocean poured blue black all around us with rose-gold shimmers from the sun. Gradually, the water mellowed to navy blue, then indigo, and finally azure, as we drew closer to the shallows. Clumps of turtle grass looked like cloud shadows on the floor. After three hours, a pale-blue ribbon appeared on the horizon and we headed toward it. Flying fish leaped near the bow and hurled themselves through the air a dozen yards at a time, like rocks skipping over the water.

Soon we entered the dreamtime of the aqua shallows. This area rises like a stage or platform in the ocean, without coral or large schools of fish. It appears to be a desert, a barren pan; but there are few places on earth without life of some sort. Here there is a bustling plant community, from simple blue-green algae to more complicated plants with stems and leaves. Plankton, the first step of the food chain, thrives on the banks, even though the waters look quite empty to the casual observer.

A bottlenosed dolphin leaped near the boat, then zoomed in and lined up with the bow, swinging back and forth like a surfer finding the sweetest spot of a wave. Soon it was joined by a second. Hobos hitching a ride, the dolphins weren't moving their tails at all, but were carried along at speed by the bow wave. They seemed to relish the sport. Beautiful as these dolphins were, we were on the lookout for their cousins, the spotted ones.

A Concorde sailed through the ocean overhead, making a double *boom!* as it passed. What is speed to the passengers on that supersonic, I wondered, or to the dolphins surfing on the bow wave?

"More dolphins!" the captain cried, pointing west.

As seven spotted dolphins homed in on the boat, we donned snorkeling gear and jumped into the water with them. A mother and baby accompanied by another female arrived first, swam straight up to us and started playing. A dolphin went close to one woman, waited for her to follow, then started turning tight circles with her. Like dervishes, dolphin and human spun together. Meanwhile, two other dolphins dived down to the bottom, about forty feet below, and made fast passes at me. I turned to follow them. Slowing, they allowed me to swim with them in formation, only inches away. By now the dolphins were all over us, swirling and diving, coasting close and wiggling away to see if we'd follow. If I dived, they dived, and they often accompanied me back to the surface, eye to eye. At first it was startling how close they came. We have an invisible no-man's-land around our bodies that others don't enter unless they mean to romance or harm us. To have a wild animal enter that dangerous realm, knowing that you could hurt it or it could hurt you, but that neither of you will, produces instantaneous trust. After it happens once, all fear vanishes. Somehow, they managed to keep their slender distance—as little as two or three inches—without actually making physical contact.

But they were touching in another sense, with their X-ray-like sonar, patting our skin, reaching deep inside us to our bones and soft tissues. At times, I could feel their streaming clicks. They seemed especially interested in one woman's belly. Could they tell she was pregnant? Probably. I wonder how the fetus showed up on their sonar. Could they echolocate our stomachs and know what we ate for lunch? Could they detect broken bones and tumors? Could they diagnose some diseases in us and in themselves? Hard to say. Because we couldn't touch them, they seemed aloof. But they were touching us constantly. For them, the contact was intimate, sensuous, if one-sided. What do dolphins feel when they echolocate one another?

At least we know *how* dolphins echolocate: they produce narrow streams of clicks (intermittent bursts of sound that last less than a thousandth of a second each) by blowing air back and forth through nasal passages. When the sound enters a fat-filled cavity in the head, it's focused into a single beam that can be directed wherever the dolphin wishes. First the dolphin sends out a general click, then it refines the signal to identify the object, which usually takes about six clicks, each one adjusting the picture so subtly that only chaos theory can explain it. At lightning speed, the dolphin sends out a signal, waits for the echo, decides what pulse to send next, waits for that one's echo, and so on, until it detects the object and classifies it. Some likely categories are: edible, dangerous, sexy, inanimate, useful, human, never-before-encountered, none of the above.

For an hour, the dolphins played exhausting, puppyish chase-and-tumble games. Meanwhile, we tried to study their markings. Each had a distinctive pattern of spots, tail notches, blazes. Often they darted to the sandy bottom and found silvery sand dabs that they chased and ate. They were like hyperactive children, easily bored, full of swerve and spunk. And we were their big bathtub toys. Taking a striped, pink-and-purple ribbon from the end of my long braid, I let it float within eyeshot of a dolphin. In a flash, the dolphin grabbed the ribbon, then tossed it up, caught it with a flipper, tossed it backward, kicked it with its tail, caught it with the other flipper, spun around, slid it over its nose, swam away with it, then returned a moment later and let it fall through the water like a cast-off toy. A clear invitation. Taking a lungful of air, I dived after the ribbon, grabbed it with one hand, tossed it back to my fins and flicked it with a clumsy kick. By this time I needed to resurface to breathe, so I let the ribbon drift down, undulating like a piece of kelp. The dolphin collected it at speed over the pyramid of one flipper, let it slide back to the tail, whisked it up and tossed it with the other flipper. I knew the rules of the game, but I didn't have the breath to play it. Even if I were a pearl diver and could hold my breath for over five minutes, I would still have been out of my league. After a few more of my clumsy lunges for the ribbon, the dolphin swam away, turning its attention to a human who could stay underwater longer, a man taking still photographs with a flash camera.

When at last they veered off toward the horizon, we gathered under the blue canopy to fill in sketch sheets and record the details of each animal. These rough sketches would be compared to photos of known animals, and become part of the researchers' catalogue. You'd think nine observers might supply the same facts, but we didn't all agree on what we saw. Indeed, we sounded like people comparing different versions of an accident. As I filled out sketch sheets, I scanned my memory for head, tail, and flank markings. Living mainly in the tropics, spotted dolphins have long, narrow beaks and can be heavily freckled. Like reverse fawns, the young begin life solid colored, usually gray, and only develop white spots as they age. By the time they're elderly, they're covered in swirls of spots and splotches. They grow to about eight feet long, have teeth, and are gregarious. They love to play, which they do with endless ingenuity and zest. Athletic, acrobatic swimmers, they leap into aerial pirouettes, cartwheels, and what seem like attempts to see how long they can hover in the air.

Over the next week, we encountered spotted dolphins every day, the longest session lasting three hours, so long in fact that we were the first to give up out of exhaustion, only to find the dolphins racing after us and trying to tempt us back to romp. Mother dolphins often brought the sleek little surprise of their babies, which appeared perfect and unmarked by life. Sometimes a baby would swim tucked underneath its mother, making a crescent shape, so that it looked as if the baby were still being carried inside. We grew to know them as individuals, a rare privilege. In our travels across the banks, we played with dolphins nine times. The most frequent visitor was a particularly rambunctious five-year-old female called "Nicky," and she became a special favorite. Often, the dolphins arrived like a visitation. Long hours of waiting, in a slow-motion of heat, glare, and water, were suddenly broken by the wild and delicious turmoil of incoming dolphins. When they left, everything fell calm again and we waited once more, at a low ebb, under the harrowing sun.

On our last day, after a particularly exhausting afternoon with Nicky and her friends, we gathered on the deck to watch the sunset. These were some of the most dramatic moments in each day, when the soft aqua of the water fanned through rainbow blues and was washed away in the molten lava of the setting sun. Night fell heavily, in thick black drapes. Retreating to the galley downstairs, we sat and talked about the week. Despite the mild discomforts of ocean sailing, everyone was sad the voyage was over, and all felt nourished by a week of such intimate play with wild animals. I was especially surprised by how eager the dolphins were to make eye contact. Their wildness disappears on one level and is enhanced on another when you stare straight into their eyes, realizing that these are wild creatures and there is something special happening inside their minds. At the very least, there is a willing gentleness and an awareness that draws you in. One reason the plight of the dolphin touches us is because we fear they may be self-aware, not just meaty animals but intelligent life-forms. Suppose, like us, they have inner universes? Suppose they are not like elk or salmon, but animals with a culture of sorts, animals that can judge us?

During the night, the winds kicked up and four-foot seas rolled in from the southwest. Sleeping on deck, I awakened to find that I had slid off my air mattress and my legs were suspended over the side of the boat. Hands folded on my chest, I looked set for burial at sea. So I retreated below, wedged myself into a narrow bunk, and tried to sleep, which was nearly impossible given the lurching and shuddering of the boat. My thoughts turned frequently to the dolphins. Where were they now? What were they doing in that incomprehensible darkness of sea and greater darkness of night? I was stricken both by our kinship with them and by the huge rift between us evolution has created. They were minds in the ocean long before we were minds on the land. They abide by rhythms older than we know or can invent. We pretend we can outsmart and ignore such rhythms, but in our hearts we know we're steered by them.

In all the excitement of the week, people had leaped into open ocean and swum with schools of large bullet-shaped barracudas, seen a bull shark at touchable range, watched lavender skates hiding on the sandy floor beneath them, and found frisky, hospitable dolphins everywhere. That made the ocean itself seem friendlier. Lumbering creatures of the earth, we find the ocean frightening. For most people, it is another form of night. It seems dark, endless, hostile, full of monsters ready to separate us from our cells. Dolphins leap from that world with a Mona Lisa smile. Playing recognizable games, they reassure us that the unknown may not be so hostile after all.

Throughout history, humans have been enthralled by the

dream of swimming and playing with dolphins. The urge is ancient and powerful, and often appears in religious myths. It pos-
sesses us, but why? Perhaps, in part, because it seems so much like
flight. Who hasn't felt the euphoria of flying in dreams? There is a
peace in weightlessness, a freedom that comes from breaking the
physical bonds that hold us. We are beings inextricably anchored
to the ground, who walk the earth and, in time, will become part
of it. In rare moments, or in dreams, we rise above those grim
restraints and joyously take flight. Perhaps, also, on some level,
flying recalls for us the perfect peace the embryo feels afloat in
its mother's womb. All this echoes the weightlessness we feel in
the sea, a victory over gravity symbolized by the rapture of dolphins. We want to regain that buoyancy for ourselves. Then, un-
fettered, our minds might roam more freely. "To halt and hang
attached to nothing, no lines or air pipe to the surface, was a
dream," Jacques Cousteau writes of his ocean dives. "At night
I often had visions of flying by extending my arms as wings. Now
I flew without wings." We know dolphins are intelligent, perhaps
as intelligent as we humans. In Shark Bay in Western Australia,
for example, dolphins have been seen carrying sponges on the
tips of their snouts. Researchers think the dolphins are using the
sponges to protect their noses from spines and stings as they hunt
food on the seabed, and dragging sponges in the sand to flush out
potential prey. And there is that fixed smile. Although it's an
anatomical accident, not a voluntary expression, it makes them
look as if they might be having more fun than we stodgy folk
above the waves. Small wonder people credit them with brain-
power, spirituality, and deep emotions. Aristotle even claimed
that dolphins speak like humans, and "can pronounce vowels . . .
but have trouble with consonants."

We sometimes picture dolphins as cherubic creatures, or benign space aliens, a New Age emblem of otherworldly innocence.
But they're also seen as powerful shamanistic envoys. Dazzling as

they leap from the thick churning water into the sheer invisibility of air, they seem immune to boundaries, magical in flight. They transcend natural prisons. They bridge worlds. Dolphins are often portrayed as seers and savants who can peer into our hidden depths, those dark emotional oceans inside our psyches. To some, they dwell in a world of crystals and spirit guides. To others they allow us a transmigration of souls. In cultures as varied as Greek, Inuit, and that of the Australian Aborigines, art and myth show dolphins saving people, guiding ships to safety, playing with swimmers, having a special kinship with humans. In Belém, on the Amazon, one can find river dolphin vulvas and penises for sale in the voodoo market. But on most of the Amazon the pink dolphins are protected by elaborate myths and no one hunts them. Like the silkies of Scottish legend, dolphins are thought to come ashore and make love with women from time to time. So an illegitimate child is said to be the child of a dolphin, and if you kill a dolphin you may be killing your own father. In Native American myths, dolphins are messengers from the Great Spirit. In Arabian tales dolphins accompany the souls of the dead to the underworld. To early Christians, a dolphin draped over a cross symbolized Christ. The Minoans revered the dolphin, proclaiming it an incarnation of their sea god, Poseidon. Born of Apollo (the sun) and Aphrodite (love), it connected the blazing sky with the fertile sea. In Greek, the words "dolphin" (*delphis*) and "womb" (*delphys*) sound alike. Say *dolphin,* and be reminded of the womb of the sea; say *womb* and be reminded of the spirit of the dolphin connecting male and female, heaven and earth. Greek and Roman mythology abounds with gods and goddesses, sailors and other mortals, being transformed into dolphins. Thanks to Apollo, a dolphin even swims across the night sky as the constellation Delphinus. Ovid tells the story of Arion, a seventh-century B.C. poet and musician, born on the isle of Lesbos, who traveled throughout the kingdom, singing and playing the lyre. Returning home

from Sicily with his earnings, he was robbed by sailors who intended to kill him. Arion asked to sing one last song before he
was murdered, and permission was granted. His poignant music
traveled across the waves, attracting a school of dolphins who
encircled the boat. Arion leapt overboard into their midst and a
dolphin carried him on its back to shore. There he reported the
thugs, who were captured and punished. A great lover of poetry
and music, Apollo was so pleased with Arion's triumph that he
placed the dolphin and the lyre among the constellations.

Dolphins, running before the bow of a ship, connect the
worlds of water and air so deftly that they seem at times to be not
only spirit guides, but ambassadors who might somehow inter-
cede between us and the rest of nature. Perhaps there is a need in
us to feel accepted by dolphins on behalf of nature, a need for a
spiritual experience, a need to reassure them out of a sense of collective guilt that we mean them well. Finding a way back into an
intimate relationship with nature may well be the essence of our
age-old dolphin dreams. But what are we to make of dolphins
and humans *playing* together, seemingly with equal abandon? Dolphins choose to play with us when they find us in their waters,
but we travel long distances and endure considerable hardship
to make that communion possible, to enjoy deep play with wild
animals. On returning from such pilgrimages, people speak like
mystics of the transcendence they felt and the transforming
beauty of the ocean, which they describe as a sacred realm.

CHAPTER THREE

Sacred Places

There are no more deserts. There are no more islands. Yet one still feels in need of them. To understand this world, one must sometimes turn away from it; to serve men better, one must briefly hold them at a distance. But where can the necessary solitude be found, the long breathing space in which the mind gathers its strength and takes stock of its courage?

—Albert Camus, *Lyrical and Critical Essays*

The perfect stillness of the night was thrilled by a more solemn silence. The darkness held a presence that was all the more felt because it was not seen. I could not any more have doubted that *He* was there than that I was. Indeed, I felt myself to be, if possible, the less real of the two.

—William James, *The Varieties of Religious Experience*

*F*rom time immemorial people have embarked on pilgrimages as a way to elevate the spirit. After a recent survey, the English Tourist Board was surprised to discover that 72 percent of all tourists said they had come to the United Kingdom to visit shrines, churches, and other holy places. Most tourists the world over are making pilgrimages either to their homelands, or to historic or religious sites such as the Greek temple of Delphi.

Built in 1400 B.C., Delphi housed the Pythian oracle, a priestess who went into trance states and foretold the future—usually in cryptic pronouncements. People from many nations flock there to this day, though paradoxically what they wish to learn is not about the future but about the past. Did the Pythian oracle really have visions? The temple was located over an active geological fault in the earth, from which petrochemical fumes seeped. According to historic accounts, the oracle inhaled this "plenum," a powerful and mysterious force from which she drew the gift of prophecy. On every continent one can find equally magical sites, usually accompanied by elaborate myth and ritual.

Half a million people each year pilgrimage to the Australian outback to behold Ayers Rock, a massive dome of red sandstone rising out of the Australian desert, a site of universal sacredness to the Aborigines, who call it Uluru. Intimately connected to their land, every inch of which is holy, symbolic, and vibrating with myth, the Aborigines inhabit "the Dreaming," a complexly imagined universe that inspires and embraces them. As they conduct the normal affairs of their lives, they continually travel through that tightly woven world of knowledge, perception, moral code, and recollection, following a maze of invisible roads, or Songlines. Closest perhaps to the way in which birdsong maps out a territory, the Songlines are ancient and magical, but they are also precise map references. The continent is crisscrossed by a labyrinth of Songlines, and the Aboriginals can sing their way along them. Bruce Chatwin describes the process in *The Songlines:*

Regardless of the words, it seems the melodic contour of the song describes the nature of the land over which the song passes. So, if the Lizard Man were dragging his heels across the salt-pans of Lake Eyre, you could expect a succession of long flats, like Chopin's "Funeral March." If he were skipping up and down the MacDonnell escarpments, you'd have a series of arpeggios and glissandos, like Liszt's "Hungarian Rhapsodies."

Certain phrases, certain combinations of musical notes, are thought to describe the action of the Ancestor's *feet*. . . . An expert songman, by listening to the order of succession, would count how many times his hero crossed a river, or scaled a ridge—and be able to calculate where, and how far along, a Songline he was.

To the Aborigines, geography is memory. Every mile sings, every mountain speaks of their ancestors' journeys. Nothing is irrelevant, nothing is lost to death. All things partake of life's spirit and vitality, the land is vigorously alive, unseen forces flourish, and all have a special site (or Dreaming Place) that is a spiritual home for them and their ancestors. The following plea for land rights, by Gulawarrwuy Yunupingu and Silas Roberts, chairmen of the Northern Land Council, offers a beautiful definition of the Dreaming:

Aborigines have a special connection with everything that is natural. Aborigines see themselves as part of nature. We see all things natural as part of us. All things on earth we see as part human. This is told through the idea of the *dreaming*. By dreaming we mean the belief that long ago, these creatures started human society; they made all natural things and put them in a special place. These dreaming creatures are connected to special places and special roads or tracks or paths. In many cases the great creatures changed themselves into sites where their spirits stayed.

My people believe this and I believe this. Nothing anybody says to me will change my belief in this. This is my story as it is the story of every true Aborigine.

These creatures, these great creatures, are just as much alive today as they were in the beginning. They are everlasting and will never die. They are always part of the land and nature as we are. We cannot change nor can they. Our connection to all things natural is spiritual. We worship spiritual sites today. We have songs and dances for those sites and we never approach [them] without preparing ourselves properly. When the great creatures moved across the land, they made small groups of people like me in each area. These people were given jobs to do but I cannot go any further than that here.

It is true that people who belong to a particular area are really part of that area and if that area is destroyed they are also destroyed. In my travels throughout Australia, I have met many Aborigines from other parts who have lost their culture. They have always lost their land and by losing their land they have lost part of themselves.

I think of land as the history of my nation. It tells of how we came into being and what system we must live. My great ancestors who lived in the times of history planned everything that we practise now. The law of history says that we must not take land, fight over land, steal land, give land, and so on. My land is mine only because I came in spirit from that land and so did my ancestors of the same land. . . .

My land is my foundation. I stand, live and perform as long as I have something firm and hard to stand on. Without land . . . we will be the lowest people in the world, because you have broken down our backbone, taken away my arts, history and foundation. You have left me with nothing.

What a statement of faith that is, passionately felt and undeniably candid. How does one begin to describe—let alone legitimize—the core of one's spirituality? Intricately stitched into a landscape every particle of which is holy, the Aborigines regard Ayers Rock as the most hallowed spot of all. So it's no surprise that the government turning their land into a tourist mecca has led to battle. "How can Mr. Court say that his Government owns this country?" Fred Forbes, chairman of the Ngaanyatjara Council argued in 1980. "It belongs to the Dreaming and not to him. Does Mr. Court also say that he owns the moon, and the sun and the sky?"

To accommodate and protect the tourists, the Australian government has installed handrails and fences at Ayers Rock, an improvement that the Aborigines still find disrespectful, arguing that white church members attend their own churches with reverence and would never climb over the sides and roofs of their holy buildings.

Tourists flock to Stonehenge, too, though only ghosts remain to chide the profane visitor. Most likely this famous circle of monolithic stones, dragged from distant quarries, served as a calendar of sorts, catching the moon and solstice sun in its crevices. So many people pilgrimage to Stonehenge each year that the British government has had to fence it off, lest people destroy it by chipping away at the stones for souvenirs. Plans are under way for the building of a concrete replica, and for the original to be returned to its sacred status and declared off-limits. Because it is sacred, we respect it and are eager to keep it intact. We feel that way instinctively about the sacred, despite the fact that we don't know the details of the religion that inspired either Stonehenge or many other ancient sites, or what exactly was considered holy. That the place once was sacred to many is enough to stir us.

The same is true at the Lascaux cave in France, where a laser-perfect replica stands near the original grotto, complete with paintings created with duplicates of the same pigments and techniques used by the ancients. Although they're magnificent reproductions, well worth a visit, I longed to see the original cave where about thirty thousand years ago something startling took place—art magic, probably accompanied by fearsome worship and initiation rites. In 1992, I was lucky enough to enter the original cave, an unforgettable and mystical experience.

The Cro-Magnon cave painters were about our size, and we know they traveled or had contact with nomadic tribes because shells from the Mediterranean have been found at Lascaux. They didn't live in the caves, but in rock shelters and huts near water. People created art before they did, but mainly as body decoration. For humans, at least, art is deliberate, compulsive, and ancient. Our earliest ancestors felt the need to create art. Through it, they touched the soul of creation. It was a sacred act, a form of magic. They used it to worship, teach, decorate important tools; they made representations of their gods and of their world. One day, someone must have unveiled a daring idea: to move from decorating the self to decorating surfaces of the world. Did that scare or fascinate people? Did it catch on right away, or take persuasion? The caves were holy places, places in which to paint visions and learn courage. These dimly lit, fetid tabernacles filled with dancing shadows, portraits of mythic beasts, and terrifying mazes in which to get lost, ensured a heart-pounding test of nerve. Few people would have seen the paintings, and then only by climbing down rocks, crawling through holes, and fearfully confronting wild spirits by torchlight.

Oddly enough, there are no reindeer painted on the walls, yet reindeer is what the painters mainly hunted. The animals they did paint—bison, horses, a unicorn, wild cattle—were not like the reindeer, but in some way sacred. The drawings were complex, subtle, keenly observed, full of perspective and sculptural techniques that were not formally "discovered" until the Renaissance. Present-day visitors stand and quietly regard the drawings as if in a museum. But 35,000 years ago initiates probably entered the cave with a priest or elder. In the flickering light of the oil lamps, the brightly colored animals would have seemed alive, galloping in a frenzy across the walls. People may have run through the firelit caves, swept up in a whirlwind of wild animals and dancing shadows. The animals would have loomed at the viewers: the hollows and hills of one rock form the belly and rump of a pregnant mare and the shoulders of an aurochs.

Were the paintings done on one night or over centuries? By one artist or many? Nearly 140 red sandstone lamps were found; also wicks made from juniper trees and reindeer oil for fuel. The painters used their bare hands to apply paint to large areas, manganese sticks for fine details, and moss for colors. We find the paintings powerful, but the Cro-Magnon artists may not have had our conception of art. Their paintings were practical, and they influenced the future of the tribe. Both magical and functional, they may also have been *beautiful* if they were thought to work; but our response to their beauty carries nothing of the mixture of anxiety, awe, dread, and hope they probably aroused in the Cro-Magnons. And what of the painters? Did they paint in a trance state? Did only shamans paint? Some paintings are signed with the outline of a human hand—missing finger joints. Did they sacrifice these to ensure future food and well-being, as some anthropologists suspect?

Moving backward through time, we tend to picture the Cro-Magnons as cruder, slightly dumber versions of ourselves. True, we share their emotions and instincts, but they were probably unlike us in vital ways, probably without our self-interrogating mental stew. Indeed, they may have had little sense of self in their dealings with the outside world. Paradoxically, that's what we now long for, to "lose ourselves" in our work, sports, art—to transcend and escape from the clamorings of the self, and from that infernal prediction machine, the brain. Deep play leads us away from that labyrinth of fire.

I remember climbing up the stairs from the Lascaux cave at night, and seeing distant lampposts, car lights, lights in farmhouse windows, lights in the village. A large plane, flying low overhead with windows lit, looked like a dining car in a painting by Hopper. Soon it would float above the constellations of Paris and land at Orly airport. More ancient constellations glittered overhead. Although they were randomly spaced balls of light, people throughout the world had connected them into shapes. Our eyes crave pattern, we search for the familiar. Quickly I found the North Star, which the Chinese called "the great ruler of Heaven," in the constellation Capricorn. The Aztecs pictured Capricorn as a whale, the East Indians thought it was an antelope, the Greeks saw it as "the gate of the gods," and the Assyrians as a "goatfish." Our eyes are great explainers, so we have made a map of the sky with which to navigate. Not only humans— other animals navigate by the stars, too. Charles Walcott at Cornell's Ornithology Laboratory once staged an experiment with homing pigeons in a planetarium, proving that they guide by the stars. Columbus steered by the stars. So did the Polynesians, who explored vast reaches of the South Pacific. Just as different cultures have connected the stars into different constellations, they've seen their own private dramas in the Milky Way. When they stared into the upside-down well of deep space, they saw a strange white blur and explained it in many different ways. The Kalahari bushmen called it "the backbone of night." To the Swedes, it was "the winter street" leading to heaven. To the Hebridean islanders, "the pathway of the secret people." To the Patagonians, obsessed with their flightless birds, "the white pampas where ghosts hunt rheas." As I stood atop the Lascaux stairs, I felt connected to all the nomads and navigators who ever lived, the explorers, the pilgrims, the lost wayfarers desperately trying to find their way home.

It's ironic that although Lascaux, Ayers Rock, and Stonehenge were built for the eyes of a faithful few, they've been visited by profane millions. However, most of the world's sacred places are visited not by tourists but by ardent believers. In the Black Hills of South Dakota, Lakota Indians gather in a sacred meadow each summer to celebrate *Okislataya wowahwala,* which translates as "welcoming back all life in peace." For the Chumash Indians, the rugged hills of Point Conception, north of Santa Barbara, is the western gate through which souls travel between earth and heaven. Even in the earliest writings of our kind, say in the 5,000-year-old Sumerian epic, *Gilgamesh,* we find the hero encountering a sacred stand of cedar trees. Our world is well stocked with sacred places: Mecca, Delphi, Bighorn Medicine Wheel, Mount Arafat, Lascaux, Jerusalem, Mount Sinai, the Ganges River, Machu Picchu, Niagara Falls, Lourdes, Great Serpent Mound, Mount Olympus, Stonehenge, the Great Pyramids, Mount Fuji, Mesa Verde, Canyon de Chelly, to name only a few. Many of them were built on high, beyond ordinary life, and out of most people's reach. Climbing to those lofty playgrounds, one's perspective and even one's physiology change. Self-exile, accompanied by blood pressure and breathing stresses, and a different visual field, in novel terrain, may well awaken insights or inspire visions.

Sacred places have traditionally been atop mounds and mountains, as close to heaven as possible. Mountains are symbols, reminders, visual mnemonics for the transcendental. Hard as it is to hold an abstraction in the mind, a mountain can float in the mind's eye. We are such physical beings, swathed in our senses, that we find it hard not to sense, not to brood, not to extrapolate, not to analyze, not to cling to some *thing* when we think. Nor would we wish to, since the only real stop to our

sensing is death. Yet how do we sense the unseen, powerful forces
around us? All humans have needed to personalize religion with
human faces, with buildings, objects, and sacred locales, the lofti-
est of which—by definition—have been mountains. In thirteenth-
century Japan, the Zen master Dōgen instructed his students
that "from time immemorial the mountains have been the
dwelling place of the great sages; wise men and sages have all
made the mountains their own chambers, their own body and
mind." Useful as Olympus may have been as a metaphor for transcendence, the Greeks didn't believe their gods actually lived on
that physical mountain; they regarded it as a symbol of the heavenly Olympus, a height beyond Earth's pinnacles, from which
gods looked upon human events with more perspective than
humans ever could. Thanks to all the polite fictions of subjectiv-
ity, it's impossible for us to observe ourselves with anything like
perspective, so we imagine a tribe of gods and goddesses that
can. "The intellect is characterized," philosopher Henri Bergson
writes, "by a natural inability to know life." Thus, for some forms
of knowing, we sidestep the rational. To the Pueblo people of
North America, the mountains hold the sky upon their shoulders, and divide the world into regions of mystery. The clouds are
their auras. The Apaches believe supernatural folk live in the
mountains, which provide powers to the shamans and protec-
tion to the tribe. In many Native American tribes, great teachers
are thought to live in the mountains, and before medicine men
visit them on dream journeys they must spend a night purifying
themselves with prayer and ritual.

We need holy places, kept secluded, sprung loose from
reality, separated from life's routines. Sometimes a local spot will
do, one sanctified by memory or ceremony. Other times, we're
drawn to someone else's idea of the sacred, such as Enchanted
Rock, near Fredericksburg, Texas, a smooth pate of shimmery
granite half a mile high, which the Comanches thought favored

by ghosts. At night, the ghosts spoke; one could hear their jangled voices. In 1834, a writer reported that the rock was made of platinum and held in fearful veneration by the Indians. According to legend, the last brave warriors of a now-extinct tribe died at its base. A chief is supposed to have sacrificed his daughter on one of the boulders to gain favor with the gods, who killed him instead and forced his ghost to walk the rock for eternity—this explains the footprintlike impressions in the granite. Locals still tell of a lost Spanish silver mine somewhere near the rock. If a rainbow path forms over the rock, it is said to lead to treasure. Long ago, Indians would climb to the summit in daylight, and leave offerings to the gods. But in the 1880s and 1890s local settlers also held church services there, inspired by St. Matthew's "Upon this rock I will build my church."

When a friend and I climbed Enchanted Rock last spring, in daylight and 97° heat, I didn't hear ancestral chantings. Nor would I, since the park closed at nightfall. But I knew where the legendary sounds came from: after soaking up heat during the day, the granite groans and crackles as it cools. Stress sounds—the Comanches were right about that—but geological stress, not human. Another wonderful thing about life on Earth: it's persistent. Black, teal, gray, and green lichens had covered some faces of the bare rock mound, and in unexpected spots a vernal pool gave succor to brilliant yellow flowers (coreopsis), blooming cactus and yucca, grasses, moss, algae, insects, and transparent fairy shrimp. A unique species, the rock quillwort, homesteaded the small, temporary pools. At the summit, where the sun stung and the hot wind blew, a large live-oak tree had struck root and found enough scant dirt in which to grow. How did the dirt get there, so high up, on bald rock, and so exposed? It must have accumulated grain by grain, over thousands of years. Shallow bowls catch rainwater. In those minute and fragile gardens, even small hickory trees grow and produce a crop of nuts. Over a hundred species of plants manage to grow on the granite knob, attracting lizards, snakes, insects, and birds. So Enchanted Rock has become a rare ecosystem.

Warm winds from the Gulf of Mexico swerve upward when they hit the rock, producing vigorous updrafts that vultures like to ride, over and over, just for fun. Some fundamentalists might argue that the vultures aren't really playing, but are engaged in automatic behavior provoked by various stimuli. The same folk would argue that, when dolphins leap and splash, what they're really doing is dislodging parasites. The crows dropping pebbles onto a skylight, or playing log-rolling games, would be harder for them to explain, but I'm sure they'd find a way. One might not think of vultures as fun-loving creatures, but they probably enjoy a free ride on a thermal as much as dolphins enjoy riding the bow-wave of a boat. For a winged creature, flapping is routine and contributes to much of its hard work. I'll bet most animals find effortlessness enjoyable, especially if it's novel and offers interesting sensations. We certainly do. But we also enjoy extreme physical effort, such as the balancing act of safely climbing naked stone.

Enchanted Rock itself is a billion years old, part of the primordial spine of the planet. We stood awhile at the summit, looking out over the ranchlands and scrub, historic Fredericksburg eighteen miles to the south, and the flat limestone rocks of the Edwards Plateau. We could see the Willow City Loop, and the hilly, sinuous back road thick with bluebonnets, wild poppies, and other wildflowers where we had cycled earlier. It offered a spacious view of the Texas hill country, and heaven knows it had been a heart-pounding climb. Does such a large mound of granite straddle faults and contain electromagnetic lines? Granite consists of crystals, and the mound was heavily speckled with pink microcline (a kind of feldspar), chalky white oligoclase (another kind of feldspar), glassy gray quartz, and flecks of black mica. A billion years ago, the dome was molten magma seven miles deep blasting to the surface. Who can say what force fields it has created?

A spot may become holy because of its antiquity or history of miracles. In the windswept wilds of Patagonia stands a shrine of Coca-Cola bottles. Dedicated to Mary Magdalen, it celebrates a time before cars, when a weary traveler, dying of thirst, found there a discarded Coca-Cola bottle filled with enough water to save her life. Now the path has become a seldom-used road for cars, and drivers stop to say a prayer and leave a bottle of water as an offering.

Many sacred places are houses of worship: churches, temples, or shrines. Some are spots generally renowned for their spiritual intensity, sites said to focus cosmic powers; they may be ancient astronomical observatories such as Stonehenge or Chaco Canyon. Still others are burial sites, such as the Great Pyramids. Flowers found buried with Cro-Magnon dead 35,000 years ago suggest funeral rites among early hominids. In India, despite the health hazard, the Ganges River is a holy repository of the ashes of the dead. There are also sacred springs and meadows, where sunrise or the solstice may be celebrated, sacred mountains and rocks for receiving dreams or offering sacrifices. There are hot springs, sweat lodges, baptismal waters, and baths where one performs rituals of cleansing and renewal. There are sacred petroglyphs, carvings of the White Mare, stone phalluses, and other fertility sites. There are waterfalls and groves. There are regions, like Bear Butte in the Black Hills of South Dakota, which are visited for vision quests. There are mammoth sacred places, sometimes sprawling across hundreds of miles, whose pattern can only be seen from the air. The best-known of these are the Peruvian Nazca lines, which stretch for dozens of miles, depicting spiders, snakes, and miscellaneous other animals. (Erich von Daniken claimed they were drawn for the pleasure of godlike extraterrestrials who were visiting the planet.) The Great Serpent Mound, in Ohio, is the largest serpent effigy in the world. Its earthen coils stretch from open mouth at one end to tail at the other, and some anthropologists believe it may refer to solar eclipses. It's not a burial site, and its pattern isn't apparent from the ground. The same is true of many huge, sprawling 10,000-year-old earthworks following the Colorado River. Why ancient humans built them we can only guess. Humans look up to their gods, so the colossal earthworks were undoubtedly constructed over many years with a god's-eye view in mind. When we were little, *up* was the world of parents, those powerful beings who warned, praised, taught, fed, and judged us. Small wonder we think gods live on mountaintops or in the sky. Most tribes mythologize the sun, moon, and stars. Indeed, Cherokee myth says their tribe originated in the constellation Pleiades.

There are also natural wonders, sacred because they magnetize people, wrench from them profound feelings of awe and fright. What is sacred goes far beyond the religious. Rudolf Otto laments that we now use the words "holy" and "sacred" in an entirely different way from our ancestors. For us, those words mean something like "good" or "virtuous," implying religiosity and a moral code. Otto argues that, originally, what was truly sacred contained darkness as well as light, fear as well as wonder, and was not religious, but the powerful emanation one experiences at special sites. Such places trigger in us an altered state of awareness, a shift in consciousness to a profound sense of spirituality, excitation, and emotional intensity. One's senses work better; the world looks clearer, crisper, more detailed. One feels part of a larger whole. Deep play happens. Sacred places seem to catapult people into this pedestal state. They awaken a sense of oneself in the universe, they kindle ecstasy. The idea of the holy existed long before

religions were founded. It is an innate response to the simultaneously mysterious, startling, immense, overpowering, aweful, and
majestic universe. As Otto reminds us,

> [t]he feeling of it may at times come sweeping like a gentle
> tide, pervading the mind with a tranquil mood of deepest
> worship. It may pass over into a more set and lasting attitude
> of the soul, continuing as it were, thrillingly vibrant and reso-
> nant, until at last it dies away and the soul resumes its "pro-
> fane," non-religious mood of everyday experience. It may
> burst in sudden eruption up from the depths of the soul with
> spasms and convulsions, or lead to the strangest excitements,
> to intoxicated frenzy, to transport, and to ecstasy. It has its
> wild and demonic forms and can sink to an almost grisly hor-
> ror and shuddering. It has its crude, barbaric antecedents and
> early manifestations, and again it may be developed into
> something beautiful and pure and glorious. It may become
> the hushed, trembling, and speechless humility of the crea-
> ture in the presence of—whom or what? In the presence of
> that which is a *mystery* inexpressible and above all creatures.

The extraordinariness of the sacred, the way in which it swerves
powerfully away from ordinary life, is part of its enchantment.
Where should one go to find the sacred manifesting itself? Remote places do admirably. Naturalist John Muir often describes
his ecstasies in the wilderness, including one day in Yosemite
when he climbed a tree in a thunderstorm and was thrilled to be
flung around the sky:

> Never before did I enjoy so noble an exhilaration of motion.
> The slender tops fairly flapped and swished in the passionate
> torrent, bending and swirling backward and forward, round
> and round, tracing indescribable combinations of vertical and

horizontal curves, while I clung with muscles firm braced,
like a bobolink on a reed.

The painter J.M.W. Turner also liked to be swallowed up by the
elements—he would strap himself to the mast of a boat and be
transported into the heart of a storm at sea, which he would later
paint in tumultuous heavings and sobbings of color.

Once, on a train through Siberia, Laurens van der Post
looked out the window at the huge expanse of flat country and
endless sky. "I thought I had never been to any place with so
much sky and space around it," he wrote, and he was especially
startled by "the immense thunder clouds moving out of the dark
towards the sleeping city resembling, in the spasmodic lightning,
fabulous swans beating towards us on hissing wings of fire." While
watching the distant summer lightning from the train, his Russian friend explained that they had a special word in Russian for
just that feeling: *zarnitsa*. The Salish Indians name the state *skalali-
tude*. The Lakota Indians use the word *skanagoah* to capture "the
still, electrifying awareness one experiences in the deep woods," a
feeling of highly attuned balance. On the slopes of Mount Kilimanjaro, Carl Jung felt an ecstatic sense of harmony with the
land, a timelessness, a vaunting self-centeredness, a belief in the
totality of his power that didn't feel egotistical at all but far-
ranging, reverent, and majestically creative:

Standing on a hill in the East Africa plains, I saw herds of
thousands of wild beasts, grazing in soundless peace, beneath
the primeval world, as they had done for unimaginable ages
of time. And I had the feeling of being the first man, the first
being to know all this. The whole world around me was still
in the primitive silence and knew not that it was. In this very
moment in which I knew it, the world came into existence,
and without this moment it would never have been.

As Jung found, some landscapes fill us with such awe that they instinctively touch a transcendent nerve. For example, there is a
natural wonder that draws millions of pilgrims every year and
fills them all with similar emotions—regardless of culture, language, or religious upbringing. I've been drawn to that natural
wonder, too, and felt the same flood of awe, reverence, and
grandeur. One day, I decide to fly deep into its mazes.

Nothing prepares you for the visual thrill of sailing over the rim,
moving suddenly from a state of flatland predictability into one
of limitless depth, change, and color. All at once we are down
into its jungles of rock, plunging toward sheer crevices, skim-
ming limestone jags by only a few yards, then swooping down
even farther to trace the winding path of the Colorado River,
rocketing up toward a large butte, wing left, wing right, as we
twist along the unraveling alleyways of rock, part of a spectacle
both dainty and massive. Who could measure it, when we are the
only certain size moving through the mazes? Off one wingtip, a
knob of limestone curves into arrowhead edges and disappears at
the base of a half-shattered tree whose open roots catch the sunlight in a cage of iridescence.

Back on land, I begin to explore the Grand Canyon on foot
from lookouts and trails along the rim. As a park for the senses,
the Grand Canyon ranks high. But in the strictest sense it is also a
playground. Sacred places are playgrounds for deep players. Or,
to put it another way, whenever one is enraptured by deep play
the playground itself becomes sacred. In both cases, special rules
must be followed; these may be cricket's rules of play at Lord's
famous ground in London, or they may be spiritual or religious
rituals. As with all games, a certain air of secrecy reigns. Time
shrinks as one gets caught up in the game. The whole universe,
perfectly contained in that one place, feels harmonious and

makes sense. Society's laws give way to higher and more urgent ones. This happens in a site limited by time and space, a world that exists inside ordinary life, but removed from it. A sacred place is a playground, the temporary home of one's exaltation, where one travels to find rapture in what is essentially an open-air seminary of the mind.

Hypnotized by the intricate vastness, I hike from one triangulation point to another, finding two of the ninety bronze survey disks that were installed decades ago by the Boston Museum of Science/*National Geographic* expedition. Sitting alone on a plinth jutting far over the emptiness, I listen to the monumental silence and find my mind roaming over the notion of wonder. The canyon, in part, is a touchstone to other wonders, revealing the uncanny work of erosion, a great builder of landscapes; five geologic eras piled one on top of the other like Berber rugs; the evolution of life viewable in a fossil record; and the fumings of the Colorado River (whose color changes during the year from deep green to bright red, or even to milky blue). Gigantic as the canyon is—217 miles long—it is the world in miniature: seven environments (from Sonoran to Arctic Circle); desert barrenness to spring lushness. It is certainly the grandest American cliché, explored by many but an enigma nonetheless. No response to it seems robust enough.

In a world governed by proportion—in which the eye frames a moment, digests it, frames another—scale is lost; visual scale, mental scale, emotional scale. If your lips purse in a silent *wow!* at the sight of Niagara Falls, what is suitable here, where your heart explores some of its oldest dwellings? The mind makes its own lavish prisons; rarely does one confront in nature a prison unimaginable. How can you explain an emptiness so vast and intricate, an emptiness rare on this planet? Not the sprawling, flat, oddly clean emptiness of a desert or arctic region, but an emptiness with depth. There are no yardsticks, unless one is lucky enough to catch sight of a dark speck moving along the canyon floor—a mule and rider. But that is part of the puzzle of this labyrinth, a maze both of direction and of scale, a maze in three dimensions.

It's easy to forget how ugly nature often seemed to people before Romanticism reexplored the unevenness of natural beauty. Early nineteenth-century writers found the canyon grotesque—not just dangerous and obstructive and rife with bloodthirsty Indians, but actually a vision of evil. C. B. Spencer described it as "Horror! Tragedy! Silence! Death! Chaos! . . . a delirium of Nature," while another writer called it "the grave of the world." After two world wars and assorted smaller ones, with all the atrocities attendant on them, it's no longer possible to find works of nature horrible, tragic, deadly, chaotic; humankind has personalized those traits forever. Now the canyon is just the opposite: a sanctuary, an emblem of serenity, a view of innocence.

The Cárdenas expedition of 1540 discovered the canyon for the Caucausian world but felt no need to name it. For three hundred years it was too overwhelming to report except in whole phrases and sentences. And then in the 1850s and 1860s "Big Cañon" and "Grand Cañon of the Colorado" came into use, as if it were *one* of anything. For it is not one but thousands of canyons, thousands of gorges and buttes, interflowing, mute, radiant, changing, all with a single river among them, as if joined by a common thought.

In the canyon's long soliloquy of rock, parrots of light move about the grottoes and real swifts loop and dart, white chevrons on each flank. The silence is broken only by the sound of air whistling through the gorges, and the occasional whirring of a helicopter. Now and then one hears the sound of a furnace whumping on: a bird taking flight. There is no way to catalogue the endless dialects and languages and body types of the tourists encountered at the rim. With binoculars as various as they are,

visitors search the canyon for trails, mules, signs of other people.
The need to humanize the marvel is obsessive, obvious, and universal. With glass lenses extending real eyes, canyon visitors become part of the evolution on show. If we cannot go backward in
time, we can at least creep into it, above desert floors and red-rock
mesas and ponderosa pine, then suddenly slip over the rim of
dreams and down through the layers of geological time.

What is *grandeur* that it should form rapidly in the mind when
one first sees the Grand Canyon? Why do we attach that concept
to this spectacle? Is it merely the puniness of human beings compared with the gigantic structures of rock? The moon, the biggest
rock most of us know, has been domesticated in literature and
song, but the canyon has resisted great literature. As with the
universe and the workings of nature, there is no way to summa-
rize it. The ultimate model of a labyrinth, it is gargantuan and
cryptic, full of blind alleys and cul-de-sacs. We are compulsive ar-
chitects; to see engineering as complete, colossal, and inimitable
as this—still far beyond our abilities—is humbling indeed. As
John Muir said in 1896, upon first viewing the canyon: "Man seeks
the finest marbles for sculptures; Nature takes cinders, ashes,
sediments, and makes all divine in fineness and beauty—turrets,
towers, pyramids, battlemented castles, rising in glowing beauty
from the depths of this canyon of canyons noiselessly hewn from
the smooth mass of the featureless plateau."

Most of all, the canyon is so vastly uninvolved with us, with
mercy or pity. Even the criminal mind is more explicable than
this—a quiddity we cannot enter, a consciousness that does not
include us. We pass through much of our world as voyeurs and
yet we are driven, from sheer loneliness, I suppose, to attribute
consciousness to all sorts of nonconscious things—dolls, cars,
computers. We still call one another totemic names by way of en-
dearment; we would like to keep the world as animate as it was
for our ancestors. But that is difficult when facing a vision as

rigidly dead as the Grand Canyon. It is beautiful and instructive and calming, but it is also the absolute, intractable "other" that human beings face from birth to death, the sharp counterpoint to our lives.

Perhaps that's why tourists mainly respond to it with a long pause of recognition, the momentary twisting of a brow as they try to construe it, and then a long, slow silence while they sit and behold it—a vast incomprehensible landform that both humbles and exalts—until their bus must go, or the fading light leaves the thinnest catwalk between the blue sky and the bluer outlines of rock.

Consciousness is the great poem of matter, whose opposite extreme is a Grand Canyon. In between, matter has odd fits and whims: lymph, feathers, brass. Cactus strikes me as a very odd predicament for matter to get into. But perhaps it is no stranger than the comb of an iris, or the way flowers present their sex organs to the world, or the milky sap that often oozes from inedible plants. There is something about the poignant senselessness of all that rock that reminds us, as nothing else could so dramatically, what a bit of luck *we* are, what a natural wonder.

At the South Rim, brass sighting tubes make arbitrary sense out of the vista. Lay the lensless tube into a slot marked "battleship" and there will be a facsimile in rock. The other sites are mainly temples: Vishnu Temple, Wotan's Throne, Zoroaster Temple, Brahma Temple, Buddha Temple, Tower of Ra, Cheops Pyramid, Osiris Temple, Shiva Temple, Isis Temple, and so on. One of the most dramatic, tall, and precarious buttes is referred to as "Snoopy" because, they say, it resembles the cartoon dog lying on his doghouse. All this demotion of the spectacle troubles me. Why define a site with another site that is smaller and in some cases trivial? Why vulgarize it with pop culture icons? The word *vulgar* didn't originally mean to debase or cheapen, but to make suitable for the common people (from the Latin *vulgus*). Do

visitors to the canyon really need to have it tamed before they can
appreciate it? Nothing can compare with the Grand Canyon, and
that is part of its true marvel and appeal.

It was John Wesley Powell who, in 1860, gave the salient
buttes their temple names. To Native Americans, it did indeed
contain sacred places. Now that the gods who instructed us are
remote, we are quite obsessed with temples. We have moved our
gods farther and farther away, off the planet, into the solar system, beyond the Milky Way, beyond the Big Bang. But once upon
a time, when time was seasonal, the gods were neighbors who
lived just across the valley on a proscribed mountain. Their deeds
and desires were tangible; they were intimates.

Today on the Hopi mesas close to the Grand Canyon, in rituals older than memory, people still dress as kachinas—garish, ex-
pressionist re-creations of the essences of their world. There is a
kachina of meteors, and maize, and water vapor. In the winter
months the kachinas dwell on the 12,000-foot slopes of Hum-
phreys Peak, and in the growing season they come down to move
among humans. The Hopi have traditionally traveled into the
canyon to perform some of their rituals, and there is a spot on the
bank of the Little Colorado where, they believe, humans may
first have entered the world. Indeed, the whole area around the
Grand Canyon is full of religious lore and natural wonders. The
volcanic field just north of Flagstaff is the largest in the United
States, and flying over it you can see where the black paws of lava
stopped cold. The aerial turbulence at midday evokes the early
turbulence from which the canyon was partially formed, and
long before that the chaos of the Big Bang. Pluto was first sighted
from the Lowell Observatory in Flagstaff, in 1930. In half a dozen
other observatories in Arizona, astronomers cast their gaze upward while, close by, a million tourists cast theirs down into the
gorge.

There would be no canyon as we perceive it—subtle, mazy,

unrepeating—without the intricate habits of light. For the canyon traps light, reveals itself in light, rehearses all the ways a thing can be lit: the picadors of light jabbing the the horned spray of the Colorado River; light like caramel syrup pouring over the dusky buttes; the light almost fluorescent in the hot green leaves of seedlings. In places the canyon is so steep that sunlight enters it only briefly at noon; the rest is darkness. Mysticism begins in semidarkness and silence. Like a sanctuary of colossal proportions, the canyon thrills with vestigial darkness, vaulted arches where sunrise trembles, and forest glades filled with dapplings of light.

It is hard to assimilate such a mix of intensities; it is too close to the experience of being alive. Instead, we order it with names that are cozy, trendy, or ancient. It is like the conscious mind, smitten with thought, whose crevices spread open silently before us. Available, viewable, definable, reducible to strata of limestone and fossil, they are still mysterious crevices, still unknowable, still overwhelming, still ample and unearthly, still the earth at its earthiest.

The Douglas firs appear under, around, between, through every place one looks; they survive the rock. Many of their twisted, lightning-licked limbs are still in leaf. The cottonwoods, growing over a hundred feet tall, can use more than fifty gallons of water each day. There are a thousand kinds of flower and bird and squirrel species indigenous to the canyon (some nearly extinct). And endless numbers of otters, skunks, beavers, ring-tailed cats, deer, porcupines, shrews, chipmunks, rats, and wild burros. In the low, common desert of the inner canyon depths, only the prickly-pear cactus survives well the high temperatures and rare precipitation. It is not erosion on a large scale that has formed the canyon, but the small daily eating away of it by tiny plants and streams, reminding us what the merest trickle over limestone can achieve. From rim to floor, the canyon reveals the last two billion years of geological history and thus typifies the processes of evolution and decay in which we all take part.

But mainly there is the steep persuasion of something devastatingly fixed, something durable in a world of fast, slippery perceptions, where it can sometimes seem that there is nothing to cling to. By contrast the canyon is solid and forever, going nowhere. It will wait for you to formulate your thoughts. The part of us that yearns for the supernaturalism we sprang from yearns for this august view of nature.

At nightfall, when I fly back to Phoenix, there is no canyon anywhere, just starry blackness above and moorish blackness below. Like an hallucination, the canyon has vanished, completely hidden now by the absence of light. Hidden, as it was from human eyes for millennia, it makes you wonder what other secrets lie in the shade of our perception. Bobbing through the usual turbulence over the desert, we pick our way home from one cluster of town lights to another, aware from this height of the patterns of human habitation. Seven skirts of light around a mountain reveal how people settled in waves. Some roads curve to avoid, others to arrive. Except for the lights running parallel along the ridges, people seem desperate to clump and bunch, swarming all over each other in towns while most of the land lies empty. The thick, dark rush of the desert below, in which there is not one human light for miles, drugs me. Looking up drowsily after a spell, I'm startled to see the horizon glittering: Phoenix and its suburbs: one long sprawling marquee. Somewhere in that expanse, people enthralled by deep play will be losing all sense of time, growing tense, feeling rapture. In a blind fury, an artist may be packing—mentally or physically—for a devastating grand pilgrimage of his own.

Paul Gauguin's pilgrimage was through a Polynesia of the mind. His intense, passionate notebooks surge with solemn ideas about the raw, authentic society he would find, and with daring new projects and playful imaginings. As he navigated the vast ocean of his creativity, he sighted an oasis in the South Sea Islands, a land of replenishment, his own private Eden. Journeying to those islands fulfilled a sacred promise, and penetrating ever deeper into their interior a restless, never-ending obsession. He set off on a pilgrimage, renouncing the known world, abandoning friends and family, and traveled into a zone of ambiguity, adopting a radically different life. Such journeys usually include a sense of spiritual quest, a desire for self-knowledge and harmony with one's surroundings. However, as Abraham H. Maslow reminds us in *Religions, Values, and Peak Experiences:*

> The great lesson from the true mystics, from the Zen monks . . . is that the sacred is in the ordinary, that it is to be found in one's daily life, in one's neighbors, friends, and family, in one's back yard, and that travel may be a flight from confronting the sacred—this lesson can be easily lost. To be looking everywhere for miracles is to me a sure sign of ignorance that everything is miraculous.

Nonetheless, people obsessively plan such pilgrimages, just as Gauguin did, taking mental flights a hundred times before departure, rehearsing the protocols, sliding into the mental world of the natives, idealizing the destination, anticipating the rapture the journey's end will trigger. The pilgrimage may be briefly arduous—to the Marquesas. Or lengthy and complex—sailing blind across the Pacific in outrigger canoes. The playground may be glorified by rumor and distance, or it may be private—the sole object of a heart's imaginings. It may be civilized and full of home comforts, or it may be a dangerously exotic realm dominated by random violence and uncertainty. One's focus simultaneously narrows and intensifies. Journeying there by camel or plane may be the game, or, like Gauguin, one may prepare for years and sail across little-known seas to find the perfect arena.

At the age of forty-three Gauguin, arrived alone on the hourglass-shaped island of Tahiti on June 1, 1891, he had given up a respectable career as a suit-and-tie-wearing banker, and left behind a wife and children to devote himself to his just-budding art, which he hoped "to develop into a wild and primitive growth." He didn't know that he would turn out to be Polynesia's most famous celebrant and spend much of his life either painting or defending the rights of its citizens. An idealist, a mystic, a believer in Rousseau's vision of people achieving their best when untainted by the corrosive influences of civilization, he described himself as both "a child and a savage" who longed to "escape to a South Sea Island and live there in ecstasy and peace." Especially ecstasy. Music can express feelings directly, as pure emotion, and Gauguin hoped to do the same through such abstractions as color and shape; under the tropic sun, he painted canvases depicting luxuriant primitive scenes. He doted on women of all ages, and found in the Tahitian woman an Eve "still able to walk naked, without indecency, preserving all her animal beauty." She wears "an ironical smile upon her lips," he explained, as if describing her many incarnations in his paintings, from which "she looks at us enigmatically."

Tahiti may sound like the end of the world, a tropical destination, not a setting-off point. But Gauguin grew bored with Tahiti and, as his rapture for Polynesia itself deepened, he kept moving farther into isolation, to more remote islands, explaining simply that it was because they were cheaper. It seemed he was constantly searching for the cheapest place of all, where food was virtually free. He may have used the mercantile language of capitalist society to explain this compulsion, but at a certain point such a search for the place of ultimate inexpense leads to either paradise or death. He found both in the Marquesas, a ring of twelve steeply volcanic islands about 740 miles northeast of Tahiti. Centrally isolated, they lie farther from all continents than any other island group in the world—2,500 miles southeast of Hawaii, 3,500 miles west of Peru. They are part of French Polynesia almost by accident (an American naval officer claimed them for the United States in 1813, but President Madison, in a lapse of tropical imagination, said he didn't want them; with a flourish, France claimed them in 1842). They are where Gauguin went in his final days, to shed the last threads of western society, find rapture, and paint beneath the amber fires of the sun.

For the longest time, the origin of the Polynesians was a mystery. The islands are so small and remote, and the Pacific is larger than all the earth's continents put together. When Europeans first saw the Pacific, all of its 10,000 islands had already been discovered by a great seafaring people who had no technology, no written history. Captain James Cook spent twelve years exploring Polynesia's many jewellike islands. A sensitive observer of the peoples, he commissioned artists to record their customs, and found that inhabitants of islands as far-flung as Hawaii and the Marquesas spoke similar languages, danced the same dances, drew the same designs in their artwork, and shared religious myths. Where could they have come from? Strong wind and water currents run from east to west, and so one theory is that they drift-sailed from South America. In 1947, Thor Heyerdahl decided to prove this theory, sailing with a five-man crew on a balsa-wood raft, the *Kon-tiki,* from South America. Ninety-three days later he sighted land in the Tuamotos, proving that drift voyages between South America and Polynesia were theoretically possible.

But this was contrary to the intuitions of Captain Cook, who argued that the Polynesians were so expert in navigation that they might have sailed against the winds and currents and come from Asia. He had personally spoken with navigators who made trips of hundreds of miles between tiny islands.

Now scientists have proved that Cook was right. An early seafaring people traveled to some of the eastern islands of Polynesia from the Bismarck Archipelago, near New Guinea, about 3,000 years ago. At about the time of Christ, they sailed eastward to Tahiti and the Marquesas. They fished, raised crops, pigs, and chickens. From that home base, they launched more ambitious voyages south to New Zealand, east to Easter Island, and north to Hawaii. Their huge outrigger canoes were carved from breadfruit trees, with woven palm leaves for sails. They made "sennit" from coconut fibers—a sturdy, coarse rope that adheres to itself and is excellent for lashing canoes together. They waterproofed the seams with heated breadfruit sap, and in these voyaging canoes they carried family, livestock, and belongings. On Polynesian islands, archaeologists have found obsidian, glitter (probably for body paint), and chert that aren't indigenous to these islands but can be found on islands near New Guinea. How terrifyingly seductive such trips must have been to the ancient navigators. Forsaking everything they knew and loved, trusting their fate to the gods, gambling that they were smart enough, strong enough, brave enough to outwit death, they must have been ecstatic nonetheless, and set off amid jubilant cheers and ardent prayers. Their Everest was horizontal, not vertical. Today sailors gain accolades if they cross the Atlantic solo, accompanied by radios and navigation aids, knowing full well what waits on the distant shore. The ancient navigators sailed straight into the mouth of the unknown, wagering all.

It's hard to imagine the scale of such epic voyages over open ocean for as far as 4,000 miles. How did the Polynesian navigators find their way over the galloping swells of the misnamed Pacific?

This mystery went unsolved for the longest time. The secret details of navigation were sacred, and closely guarded by the priestly caste of navigators, who were second in importance only to the king. Every island had navigators. Now we know that they relied on a complex knowledge of the ocean, the weather, and the birds and sea creatures.

In this survival game whose skills were entrusted to only a lucky few, initiates combined mythology, religious practice, and all the excitement of a quest for the unknown as they learned to read the ocean like a holy text. We're used to thinking of radio and television waves as carrying a lot of information, but to the Polynesians the ocean waves were richly informative, too. Waves made predictable patterns around islands, coral reefs, atolls, and channels. Waves ran in certain ways before typhoons. Rolling waves, waves changing direction, staggering waves, mounting eddies and swells all built up a detailed map of an island as yet invisible to the eye. The navigators learned that water flowing around a shore, responding to each contour, carries those features far out to sea. At night, the eddies might often have even been lit by bioluminescent sea creatures, and the swells echoing out from shore would be gently hitting the canoes like radar waves. There are many other guideposts. They knew, just as the Vikings and Phoenicians did, that land birds will always be traveling in one direction at certain times of the year. Local birds, such as boobies and gannets, could be watched and followed late in the afternoon, when their ocean-feeding would be done and they would be flying back to their island nests. Mariners often kept frigate birds to turn loose, because they were known to fly straight for land, and sometimes voyagers traveled with pigs, which could smell land at a great distance. Tall islands trail clouds like chimneys smoking in the wind. There were many colors of ocean to decipher, and the depths or proximity to land they bespeak. There was the temperature of various currents. There was the great planetarium of the sky to tell their whereabouts, time, and direction. They knew hundreds of stars by name, and which islands a star would be floating above in which season. There was the familiar movement of the Southern Cross. Fish were useful to watch, too. There were the deep-sea creatures—whales, flying fish, certain sharks—and there were the local fish that rarely strayed from their coastal niches.

In 1976, Pius Mau Piailug, one of the last surviving navigators, an inhabitant of the tiny island of Satawal, showed the world how it was done by navigating 2,500 miles over open ocean in a replica of an ancient voyaging canoe. He explained that he navigated in part by using a star compass, the secrets of which he demonstrated by arranging thirty-two lumps of coral in a circle, then recounting the rising and setting point of each star. He also consulted the complex map of the ocean waves. There were eight sets of swells that could be read. On this voyage between Tahiti and Hawaii, there was a crew of seventeen and six tons of supplies. Everything was done in the ancient way. As Mau proved, even at night or in fog, when a skilled navigator couldn't see the swells, he could nonetheless *feel* and set a course by them. This was presumably how the people came to the islands long ago.

In the bay of Atuona, on the island of Hiva Oa, one finds a small, terraced cemetery brimming with flowers and shade trees. It overlooks the beach, the boats at anchor, and the mountains rolling away into the distance. A frangipani tree full of yellow and white blossoms grows at the head of Gauguin's grave, its roots part of the grave itself. The reddish gravestone is shaped like a reclining figure holding between its knees a round stone on which PAUL GAUGUIN, 1903 has been chiseled and filled in with pink. Beside the stone, under the frangipani tree, sits a replica of one of Gauguin's statues: a woman whose knees are twisted to one side, with a dog at her feet. The islanders claim that two skeletons are actually lying in his grave. That's just enough mystery to keep tongues wagging and his roguish reputation secure. He had so many women of so many ages that his final companion could be almost anyone. If this seems a windblown and lonely place, it's also serene and full of painterly vistas on every side. Images to steer through his memory and enshrine on the playing field of the canvas. That would have pleased Gauguin. A favorite game of mine (and many other people's) is putting on the lens of someone else's sensibility, to see the world in a different light. Gauguin's, Cook's, an ancient navigator's. But, in the end, shadowing a deep player's journey—on his canvases, in his journals, along the shores he explored—teaches you less about the player than about what he loved. The trembling light on the water. The deeply saturated tones of mountain, land, and culture. The distillation of spirit.

"The mountains, each inside the other," Greek poet George Seferis writes, "are bodies hugging each other. They proceed and *complete* you. The same with the sea. This amazing thing *happens.* It is impossible for me to express this revelation in a better way. After this, whether or not you are a person has no significance. Or, the person is no longer *you,* the person is *there.* If you can, you complete it. If you can, you perform a sacred act. At this point, happiness or unhappiness mean nothing; it is a struggle that takes place elsewhere." For Gauguin, the long game of paint, pilgrimage, and passion was finished. Nine years after he began his love affair with Polynesia, and two years before his death in 1903, when he moved permanently to Atuona, Gauguin wrote of his final home: "I am satisfied, here in my solitude."

Gauguin was one kind of deep player, for whom art and adventure merged. Other adventure players may be thrill-seekers, explorers, discoverers, or even some lighter-than-air individuals who stage quests containing all these elements.

CHAPTER FOUR

Into the Death Zone

These games will be the death of me yet; the wrack and ruin, or else the salvation.... Games pared down to the blazing bare bones, to the beautiful, terrible core of it all.

—Rob Schultheis, *Bone Games*

We stand on the brink of a precipice. We peer into the abyss—we grow sick and dizzy. Our first impulse is to shrink from the danger. Unaccountably we remain.

—Edgar Allan Poe, "The Imp of the Perverse"

*S*ome of deep play's original meaning, locked in the world of pledge, danger, and fixation, is perfectly visible today. In 1996, for instance, it lured three hundred people to the base camp at Mount Everest, where many climbed into "the death zone" five miles high. Some reached the pinnacle, others turned back, and nineteen

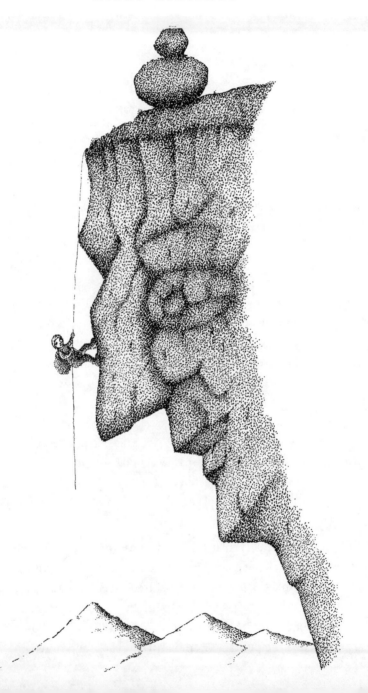

died, while a puzzled world watched. At 30,000 feet, Everest is the highest point on earth, the place closest to heaven or outer space. It's shocking to realize that Everest reaches into the jet stream, and has a permanent white contrail streaming behind it. Picturing people stumbling around in the jet stream helps to clarify why the climb is so dangerous. This season, despite reading of those agonizing deaths, even more climbers signed up, paying $70,000 each, and knowing that one in four will die. Those who do survive may lose a nose, ears, and hands to frostbite. They may face harrowing memories and jagged nightmares of the worst trauma of their lives. If they return whole, their world will seem flatter by comparison. Doing something larger than life leaves you with the rest of your less-towering days to fill. Steep thrills, by definition, begin and end with the commonplace.

It's probably no coincidence that the language of mountaineering intersects with the psychological. Climb Everest and, by general acclamation, you've amounted to something. A precipitous life, a life on the edge, proves you aren't a coward, a slacker, a weakling. Pick your way through a three-dimensional death puzzle, and no one can call you timid. Climb to the highest point on Earth, and people must look up to you. Then you are top dog, king of the hill, high and mighty, and all the other clichés that capture what height symbolizes to humans. After all, we are vertical by heritage—our primate ancestors raced up into the trees for safety and strategy. Thousands of years later, though settled and civilized, we still follow those basic instincts. It's hard to teach an old dogma new tricks. So we build high-rises, towers, and ziggurats, and we're utterly obsessed with hierarchies—who stands above whom and looks down upon whom. We still like to watch life's opera from high balconies. We climb corporate ladders, we battle for the high ground. If you can rise to the top, you become a towering and dominant figure. What lures many to Everest may be visceral, a tonic craved by muscle and imagination. Preparing for a death-defying climb can bring focus and direction to a rudderless life. But one must remember that these climbers are also staging an elaborate public display. There is a difference between private and public acts of deep play. People who climb Everest aren't quiet about it. They manage to work it into a conversation. Sir Edmund Hillary's face adorns New Zealand's five-dollar bill.

Ironically, many professional athletes aren't really playing, but working. What first attracted them to their sport may have been powerfully spiritual, but remove the voluntary, the spontaneous, the freewheeling, the transcendent, and play can quickly become earnest business. As A. Guttman insists, "Sport is not an escape from the world of work but rather an exact structural and functional parallel. . . . It seduces the luckless athlete and spectator into a second world of work more authoritarian and repressive and less meaningful" than the first. Studies have shown that if one is paid for doing what one loves, it loses some of its appeal. "Be not one whose motive for action is the hope of reward," Lord Krishna advises in the Bhagavad Gita, since happiness lies in the doing. Converting play to work usually ruins the game. However, there's also a strong tribal element in sports, which can lead to mystical states of combined purpose and sometimes to mass violence or hysteria. Wars have been fought over the outcome of soccer games.

Years ago, I decided to write a novel set in the soccer world, because I was interested even then in ceremonial violence and play. To get some atmosphere for it, I became a soccer journalist for a year. On weekends, I watched the New York Cosmos soccer matches at Giants Stadium in New Jersey. The Cosmos had attracted the world's legendary players and put them all on one team, and it was exhilarating to watch such mastery. Although each of the players was a dazzling soloist, they spoke different physical dialects, and so sometimes they didn't blend into a winning team. Each had a distinctive style, born of his culture and personality; and what is style but a playing with possible forms? I'll never forget Pelé's farewell game. He stood at the center of the stadium, surrounded by 40,000 adoring, teary-eyed fans. His voice over the loudspeaker reverberated as if it were echoing around a canyon as he said: "Repeat after me: LOVE . . . love . . . LOVE . . . love . . . LOVE . . . love."

My relationship with soccer was deep play, but many of the players I met felt quite sober and businesslike about the game. Amateur athletes and fans most often expressed playfulness and rapture. We forget that the word *amateur* means lover. In ancient times, when sports were part of religious holidays, they were holy events with cosmic significance. All that has changed, except perhaps when the Olympics become politicized, as they often do.

Today, most people don't play sports professionally, or as enthusiastic amateurs, but to achieve practical goals. People work at play. In a puritanical panic, they dismiss play as inefficient, a waste of time. According to a recent survey, people have an average of only sixteen hours of leisure time per week. In our do-more-in-less-time world, one can't afford to play unless it accomplishes something.

This attitude looms in sports magazines, which are dominated by articles about how to be more competitive. The advertisements promise their products will make one tougher and more macho. Here's a typical one in a cycling magazine: a full-page ad shows a man upside down on a snowboard, about twenty feet in the air, over rocky and snowy terrain. Atop the photo a banner reads:

BUY A PIONEER CAR STEREO NOW.

Below the photo another banner completes the thought:

BECAUSE SOMEDAY YOU'LL BE DEAD.

Next we find: "Are those 30 CDs in your pocket or are you just happy to see me?" At last a text describes the disc player for sale—but only in terms of power, loudness, and domination. Nowhere does it say how the music might sound. Presumably musical enjoyment is not the point. Another full-page ad shows a cyclist on an empty highway speeding toward the camera. His eyes are riveted straight ahead. He reminds me of a bike shop employee my friend and I encountered in Charleston, S.C. We had flown in for the day, taken a cab from the airport to a bike shop downtown, rented bikes, and asked which direction held the best rides.

"Should we head east or south?" we asked the man, who seemed surprised by the question. "Do you bike the roads around here very much?"

"Oh, yeah," he said, "I bike about 100 miles a week."

I tried again. "Well, is the scenery more interesting on the east road or the south road?"

Then he said one of the saddest things I've ever heard.

"I don't look up," he said, matter-of-factly.

In another ad, a cyclist is blazing down the macadam in a rugged landscape, and he's clearly "in the zone," as athletes say. I doubt he looks up. A banner running level with his handlebars says:

SOME RELIGIONS ARE PRACTICED SEVEN DAYS A WEEK.

Then, at the bottom of the page, smaller type reads:

RAIN OR SHINE, HOT OR COLD,

MILE AFTER RELIGIOUS MILE——NOTHING KEEPS

YOU GOING BETTER THAN GATORADE. LIFE IS A SPORT. DRINK IT UP.

Cycling magazines tend to promote a rough, tough, more-macho-than-thou image. There are occasional articles addressed to women, occasional travelogues, occasional calls for civic awareness. But the outlook is usually tough-guy, and their great gods are performance and length. Pounding out a century (a 100-mile ride) is one goal; others are racing and winning. The idea of biking just for fun—not to prove you're butch or to best somebody—doesn't rate as high. Maybe one day it will, since many cyclists these days are biking for fun and fitness; competition is something they want to leave at the office. However, they do obsess about bikes, the instrument of their transcendence.

In all forms of deep play, one becomes fascinated by an "other," in whose presence one feels exaltation. That other can be a person or a god, but it can just as easily be a war, a mountain, or a bicycle. The relationship is no less devotional and obsessive. We worship an icon from afar, but we hold an amulet in our hands and touch it as we worship it. An icon is an abstract image we worship. It's separate from us. An amulet is also an image of what we worship, but we hold it, caress it lovingly, explore its features. What we're really worshiping is life, a force full of energy, surprise, growth, mystery, creativity, and power. In romantic love, holding someone close, like an amulet, discovering how life expresses itself in their words and their ways, we hold hands with what we worship, we touch and explore the sacred. In that sense, an amulet can be a beloved soccer ball or a mountain or a bike. "The bicycle also is an amulet against various disorders," Christopher Morley writes in *The Romany Stain.* "To see before one a forked meandering road, a wedge-towered Norman church in the valley, to explore the fragrance of lanes like green tunnels, to hear the whispering hum beneath you and the rasp of scythes in a hayfield, all this might well be homeopathic against passion, for it is a passion itself."

A famous Minoan painting shows three young men leaping onto and doing handstands on the back of a raging bull. Why do we need to spark up our lives with danger, and regard that as fun?

Why are the rigors and flights of daily life not stressful enough? Why do we crave stress, especially the stress of love affairs? If necessity is the mother of invention, tedium is the father of distraction. There are people for whom the thrill of competing isn't enough; they also have to risk death, injury, or grave loss of self-esteem. It's intriguing that, after doing something which may take enormous effort or be dangerous, people nonetheless rave "That was fun!"

All the evidence suggests that there is a thrill-seeking personality. People possessing it require a lot of turmoil, and actively seek heart-pounding moments. The risk-taking can be mental or physical. The mental form produces daring artists, scientists, and entertainers, as well as criminals. The physical form includes daredevils, adventurers, and test pilots, as well as bank robbers and juvenile delinquents. At the core of such cravings for a walloping good thrill is a nervous system that needs revving up to feel normal. Some people are extremely sensitive to stimuli, and prefer calming activities, but others are more sedate and don't respond much to any stimuli, physical or mental. They require extremely dramatic events to become aroused. For decades, Frank Farley and his colleagues at the University of Wisconsin have been studying the "Type-T Personality," those people with unusually flexible minds, who see problems from many angles, shift easily between the concrete and the abstract, and find offbeat solutions and insights alluring. They're drawn to ambiguity, novelty, conflict, variety, paradox. They may thrive amid the daily terrors of war, but return home to the agonizing boredom of everyday life. They break rules, resist authority, sidestep structure. They play with ideas, juggle the familiar and uncertain, explore intense sensations and emotions, take risks. They tend to be highly creative—or highly destructive. Studies show that more men than women fall into this category, and that thrill-seeking tends to peak between the ages of sixteen and twenty-four.

World-class speed skater Steve McKinney was a typical Type-T personality. His mother, a jockey, fell off a horse when she was seven months pregnant with Steve, who was born prematurely as a result. Volatile, high-energy, intense, he became a superb downhill skier; but that temperament also got him tossed off the U. S. Ski Team. Then he tackled hang gliding, studied Zen Buddhism, took up rock climbing (a 100-foot fall in 1973 resulted in a full body cast). After climbing Everest without Sherpas or oxygen tanks, he hang glided down from its 21,500-foot West Ridge. Ultimately, he developed a passion for speed skiing, in which he set a downhill world record of 124 mph. Above all, he loved being "launched into a beautiful weird flight" down a glacier, and once summed up his life in mystical terms as "a search for peace at the very heart of movement. . . . I discovered the middle path of stillness within speed, calmness within fear." Reported to be aloof and angry much of the time, he explained his inner tumult as a retreat from daily routine into an ecstasy of calm and renewal. "You always lose it in society," he said. "Up in those high couloirs I have my talks with God. On that speed run, there is that little flash of peace. Clean, smooth, white . . . it's a cleansing deal." (Notice, once again, a deep player referring to purification.) Ironically, having survived a turbulent life packed with adventures and accidents (including a helicopter crash), he died at thirty-seven in one of his most passive moments, when a drunk driver crashed into the car where he lay sleeping.

Do such daredevils have a death wish? Not according to Keith Johnsgard, professor emeritus at San Jose State University in California. A skydiver, motorcyclist, and mountain climber himself, Johnsgard has an understandable fascination with the subject. For years, he has studied skiers who crave the adrenaline rush of skiing off steep cliffs and performing other equally hair-raising feats. Although such people are thought to court death, Johnsgard found the opposite: "The last thing these people want to do is stop living and having these kinds of rushes. If anything, these people have a life wish. They love life, they love to experiment with life, they want to live for another day of thrill-seeking."

Undoubtedly, some thrill-seekers are trying to shore up a crumbling sense of adequacy; and there will always be frankly foolish people who, on a whim, try to fly a plane under a bridge or sail into a hurricane on purpose. But serious, lifelong risk-takers tend to be altogether more focused, "cool, calculated, and thoughtful," according to Dr. Bruce Ogilvie, professor emeritus of psychology at San Jose State. "The idea that most high-risk athletes are disturbed is simply a myth." When Ogilvie decided to do a follow-up study of a group of professional racing-car drivers he had interviewed five years before, he was shocked to find that 37 percent of them were either dead or badly injured. If they're not disturbed, and they don't have a death wish, then where does the impetus for thrill-seeking come from?

Two independent studies reported in the January 1996 issue of *Nature Genetics* found that a different version of D4DR, a gene that affects how the brain responds to dopamine, occurs more frequently in people given to "novelty seeking." People who possess the gene tend to be more excitable, impulsive, thrill-seeking, and avid to explore the unknown. The studies were prompted by a theory of personality proposed by Robert Cloninger of Washington University School of Medicine, St. Louis, in the 1980s. His intriguing research into the genetics and neurobiology of personality traits has pointed up a link between dopamine and novelty-seeking behavior. A lot depends on the blend of genetic factors, which is why some novelty-seeking types may be asocial while others desire public acclaim. Cloninger theorizes that genetics alone doesn't determine personality, because a person's upbringing, environment, and unique experiences also deeply affect what we call "character," that evanescent mix of goals, cooperativeness, and spiritual beliefs that transcend the clamorings of the self. Meanwhile, Spanish psychiatrist José L. Carrasco has found that bullfighters tend to be 17 percent lower than most people in monoamine oxidase (MAO), an enzyme that breaks down excess dopamine and norepinephrine in the brain. Low levels of MAO are associated with depression, and one class of antidepressants works on the MAO level. Low MAO levels have been linked to a variety of personality traits and disorders, including impulsiveness, schizophrenia, suicidal behavior, and sensation-seeking. According to this theory, the dynamics of thrill-seeking are similar to those of manic-depression—thrill-seeking produces a temporary high, like taking cocaine.

"Sometimes we act not despite risk, but *because* of it," Leonard Zegans of the Langley Porter Psychiatric Institute in San Francisco observes. By channeling dangerous urges into acceptable jobs or leisure activities, one can gain a stronger ego and a sense of control. Then "actual self-destruction is not as feared as the destruction of one's sense of self." We evolved to hunt wild animals, brave the elements, and fight predators. Our bodies still quiver at the thought. Novelty excites, and fear rouses all the senses. Most people are happy to control those yearnings, or confine them to roller coasters, scream machines, and mock peril. But for others the restraints of a civilized, mainly intellectual life feel suffocating. Apsley Cherry-Garrard, the English explorer who accompanied Scott on his ill-fated trip to the Antarctic, wrote a gasp-filled book about it called *The Worst Journey in the World,* which begins like this: "Polar exploration is at once the cleanest and most isolated way of having a bad time which has been devised." He went on to ask: "Why do some human beings desire with such urgency to do such things: regardless of the consequences, voluntarily, conscripted by no one but themselves? I have tried to tell how, and when, and where? But why. That is a mystery." The Talmud offers at least one cryptic answer to the question. First it asks "Why do we fall into deep chasms?" Then it answers "So that we may rise again. Marco Pallis, a musician, entomologist, and mountaineer, gives this answer:

> Only he who has attained the summit and made himself one with it knows the solution of the mystery.... So long as there yet exists a step to be taken there are alternatives and hence there are possibilities of comparison, but at the summit all alternative routes become one; every distinction between them, and therefore every opposition, is spontaneously reconciled. The summit itself not only occupies no space, although the whole mountain is virtually contained in it, but it is also outside time and all succession, and only the "eternal present" reigns there.

No time is more tense than the intimate, ongoing present, where the truths are eternal. As Pavlov found, any novelty—however irrelevant—may distract an animal from its behavior. Instinctively turning toward the interruption, the animal becomes heart-poundingly aware. This "orienting" reflex, as it's called, alerts and arouses the animal, but also fills its senses with as much new information as possible, while blocking out any previous plans or distractions. Surprise, novelty, sudden change, conflict, uncertainty, or increased complexity instinctively trigger an animal's orienting reflex, and prepare it for emergency action. By its nature, novelty excites. By providing the unexpected, it shifts one off balance, forces one to release one's stranglehold on habits and improvise, learn new customs. This is especially true of "relative novelty," when things change just enough to be noticeable. Total novelty can seem different enough to be meaningless; radical changes can be ignored. But partial novelty makes sense up to a point, yet requires a new response, and so it has to be taken seriously. Our basic curiosity, as well as our passion for mysteries, exploration, and adventure may spring from the orienting reflex, the body's mindless response to novelty or change. Once an animal's curiosity is excited and it grows rigidly alert, the arousal doesn't quit until the animal explores the stimulus, investigates the sensory puzzle, and can rest assured that all is well. That cyclical pattern of arousal, tension, fear, suspense, followed by an important reward—relaxation of the body and a sense of quiet, safety, and well-being—offers an ancient pleasure that may lie at the heart of thrill-seeking. Death and rebirth, purification through ordeal, phantom companions appearing as guides, and out-of-the-body experiences are frequent motifs in risk-taking tales. Stretching from the bedrock of the ordinary to the pinnacle of perfection fills the risk-takers with rare confidence, strength, and omnicompetence. It doesn't always happen on every climb or flight. It only happens if it's *voluntary,* and it can take practice to locate the best field of play and master the necessary focus. As Jack Kerouac once quipped: "Walking on water wasn't built in a day."

Thrill-seeking is a passionate form of deep play, at one far end of the spectrum. Many people stop short of nerve-frazzling jolts and constant peril, but still seek the strange, the exotic, the intense. As they fine-tune the imagination for real out-of-the-body travel, they leave the trappings of self behind and pitch an outpost in a wild and mysterious country.

Perched in small gondolas beneath what look like gigantic Christmas ornaments, three teams of hot-air balloonists recently set out to circle the world. The grander the quest, the graver the danger. Hitching a ride on 100-mph jet streams, climbing to 30,000 feet at times, balloonists must fight storms, mechanical breakdowns, and hostile armies below. Although they reached the same altitude as Everest's climbers, and also wore oxygen masks, many fewer balloonists have traveled in those high halls.

One of the last great aeronautical challenges, ballooning around the world ignites our sense of adventure. Playing with quest and challenge is part of our evolutionary heritage. When we open up the footlocker of our humanity and look at the family photographs inside, it's not always easy to recognize the features. One of them is the need for quests, another to slip back into the ebb and flow of nature, still another to climb to the highest point one can, to enter the realm of the gods. In ballooning, all of those are in play. Ballooning tantalizes our psyches, and also reminds us of something we tend to take for granted: that human life changed radically, irreversibly, when we learned to fly.

Human flight is less than a hundred years old, still marvelous and puzzling as riding a dragon, yet it has transformed our lives. We no longer conduct romances as people did before planes, now that we can date and marry over many time zones. Our relationships with our families have changed: we can see them often; good-bye is not forever. We no longer fight wars mainly with our neighbors, and feel each battle on our pulses; now it's abstract, global, predicated on aerial surveillance. Because people from Australia, Puerto Rico, or Japan can now easily meet and marry people from California or Peru or China, the gene pool is changing; we won't look the way we do for long. How we earn our living has changed, how we educate our young, how we vacation, how we choose our leaders, how we think of news, how we raise crops, conduct police work, and give emergency aid. All because of our recent ability to fly. It has changed our notions of privacy, observation, and pollution, and what we mean by a pilgrimage. One of the first words we think humans spoke, recorded in Indo-European as *pleu*, meant: *It flies!* It is an ancient longing.

I must say I smile when I think of the thirty-nine-year-old psychiatrist-balloonist heading this year's Swiss team. What does he make of his devotion to soft objects ten stories tall, objects that can lose lift and fail? But perhaps symbols are the farthest thing

from his mind when he balloons. The sheer marvel of flight—
that we can teach unwieldy metal to fly with such delicacy—
continues to astonish us all. Like our ancient forebears, we too
exclaim: *It flies!* Small wonder Stone Age tribespeople of Papua
New Guinea greeted one charter pilot with bananas for his airplane and a desire to know what sex it was. The plane's wheels
were the first wheels they had ever seen.

One morning a few years ago, at Virginia Beach, I watched
pilots from Oceana Naval Base fly delta wings and F-14s, doing
scissor-edge turns and formation moves across the sky. They
were practicing for war, but that screech of metal on thought
was far, far away from the obvious fun they were having, pegging
tight turns over my parked car and filling the sky with contrails
before they returned to their aerodrome.

Like a shamanistic language, the lure of flight speaks to people in different idioms. We can blast rockets to the stars. We can
race across the sky on fixed wings. Ballooning appeals to the more
languorous and low-tech side of our nature; it's adventure in an
antique mood. Although I learned to pilot small high-winged
planes, from time to time I sampled gliders and balloons. Floating
slowly above landscape and civilization, through the fathoms of
sky, one is left breathless in a world that's curiously silent but for
the shaken blankets of the wind and the occasional sighs of hot
air. What a treat to stroll through the veils of twilight, to float
across the sky like a slowly forming thought. Flying an airplane,
one usually travels the shortest distance between two points. Balloonists can dawdle, lollygag, cast their fate to the wind, and become part of the ebb and flow of nature, part of the sky itself, held
aloft like any bird, leaf, or spore. In that silent realm, far from the
mischief and toil of society, all one hears is the urgent breathing
of the wind and, now and then, an inspiring gasp of hot air. There
are some truths about that world that are only knowable from
aloft. Flying has changed how we imagine our planet, whose

most exotic barrios are now as close as a jetway, and which we
have seen whole from space, so that even the farthest nations are
political and ecological neighbors. "If this stillness was the ultimate end of action," author and F-104 pilot Yukio Mishima writes
in *Sun and Steel,* "then the sky about me, the clouds far below, the
sea gleaming between the clouds, even the setting sun, might
well be events, things, within myself. At this distance from the
earth, intellectual adventure and physical adventure could join
hands without the slightest difficulty. This was the point that I
had always been striving towards."

But there is an even quieter playground, beyond plane or balloon, a spot high above all the weathers of the world, a realm I've
always dreamed of visiting. That's where I would pilgrimage to, if
I could, my perfect locale for deep play. In my mind's eye, I picture Earth as an oasis in the night sprawl of space, one compact
ball that contains many sacred places and all the life we know, a
beginning and an end of countless human journeys, the alpha
and omega for all of our imaginings, the container of time, and
what we mean when we say the word "whole." I long to travel
to the stars and visit other planets, but also to behold our own
world as a planet, to see the family of humankind under one star-
shingled roof. One day in 1986, with high hopes, and letters of reference from *Parade*'s editor-in-chief Walter Anderson, poet May
Swenson, and astronomer Carl Sagan, I applied for the Journalist
in Space project, and was thrilled to be chosen as a semifinalist.
However, that meant auditioning in an otherworldly locale.

I flew to Lawrence, Kansas. My curiosity about the world paced
like a wild animal in a cage. As a lifelong fan of space exploration
and a pilot, I wanted to step above the sky to where dreams are
weightless and see the round walls of my home. "Aren't you
afraid?" a wire-service reporter had asked only the day before. I'd

answered that there are things you do even though they may be frightening, not because you don't feel fear, but because knowledge is a tonic. Who can say at what stage fear becomes rapturous interest? But it does, even though one doesn't lose the fear. "Enthusiastic" originally meant being out of control and acting crazy (because possessed by a god). How could I resist seeing everyone I've ever known, everyone I've ever loved, my whole experience of life floating in one place on a single planet underneath me?

Driving through the heart of the country to the small university town of Lawrence, I admired the dark-green fields of standing grain and the deep brown corduroy of the ploughed farmlands. The screening process began in the School of Journalism, with color and black-and-white photographs, while I held my name on a placard under my chin, prison style. As they posed me with my shoulder to the camera, chin up, head tilted, I remembered when I'd last seen portraits like this—in high school yearbooks. The coy shoulder turn, the all-American smile.

In the video room, I received an envelope with a single sheet of white paper inside. "What was your response to the events of January 28?" it asked. The *Challenger* explosion. Stunned by their televised deaths, I had written a poem both mournful and eager addressed to the crew. Four months later, Kansas seemed light-years away from those events. Flooded with deep, partly explored memories, I wondered where on earth to begin. After a few minutes, the camera began rolling, my mouth began moving, and words filled the room. A cannonade of provocative questions followed:

"What commercial gain do you hope to realize from going up on the shuttle?"

"Do you think NASA is too public-relations oriented?"

After eight minutes, a young man motioned *Cut!*, and I collected my thoughts and the just-taped interview, which I carried along like the specimen it was, to take a seat in the hallway.

Sitting on a low bench, I waited as many others had before me, including one climber of Everest and a man who wished to broadcast from his wheelchair. In a moment, a TV newscaster from Houston emerged from the room. Handsome, dapper, deeply modulated, he was all grooming and packaging. A student aide walked him up and down the hallway as if he were a racehorse cooling down.

When it was my turn, I went into a long, narrow room at the far end of which stood tall windows looking out onto the campus. I could see through them to where students were playing Frisbee or hurrying to their last classes of the day, and the football team's mascot—a giant bird—was strutting across the grass. I was the last to audition, the only literary writer. During the twenty-minute interview, my examiners returned to the same key questions, so I knew what elements of my application troubled them.

"How will you ever manage to be a pool reporter?" they kept asking me. For a moment, I was dumbfounded. What was a pool reporter? I had never heard the term before. I sidestepped the question. Finally they asked me straight out: "How will you be content to relay facts to news gatherers on earth when your writing is so personal and subjective?"

They weren't looking for someone to bring insight or a finely tuned eye to the experience, but for a reporter who would relay their news. They were also uneasy about my lack of broadcasting experience: aboard the space shuttle, a reporter would be mainly electronic. Armed with samples of my work, including an on-the-senses account of watching a night launch of the space shuttle, they reminded me that I have a distinctive style.

"How will truck drivers identify with you?" they asked. At first, I wasn't sure how to answer that. For one thing, it was insulting to truck drivers. I was being sponsored by *Parade* maga-

zine, for which I regularly wrote essays on Americana, and I pre-
sumed that *Parade*'s readership of over 82 million included people
from many walks of life. For another, it ignored the urgent need
to send aloft writers and other artists of all sorts who have more
illuminating things to say about the experience than "gee whiz." I
argued that we needed to send up our keenest observers, to help
us understand as poignantly as possible what life is like in space,
what the whole earth looks like, and how much the view from
space can teach us.

Other questions focused less on what I sensed was their real
misgiving about me—that I would be thought too intellectual,
too idealistic, not an it-could-be-me-up-there American. Not
enough of a team player or a pool reporter, not someone who
could be trusted to express conventional values without interpret-
ing or commenting too readily. In short: a willing propagandist.

Then an invisible bell rang, and I left as I arrived—a face, a
name, and a yearning—and stood in a narrow hallway. They
were not ready to send up an artist. Most of the interview process
had to do with being suitable for the media. They made clear that
nothing was as important as being videogenic. What an enormous amount of energy NASA was spending on public relations.
This was why Louis Friedman, Bruce Murray, Carl Sagan, and
other astronomers had founded The Planetary Society, to lobby
for and promote the exploration of space, and why I agreed to be
a member of its advisory board. In an ideal world, we all would be
deft caretakers of our planet and solar system, unflagging cele-
brants of life's variety, and bold inquirers into the startling
universe we both navigate and find ourselves at sea in. I knew
The Planetary Society didn't believe it could single-handedly
achieve that alchemy of mind, from the baseness depicted in the
news everyday to the gold of a renewed sense of wonder, awareness, and responsibility. But it offered the right attitude for us to

follow. We are beings whose hallmark is the ability to marvel. So I was pleased to be associated with its sense of celebration and inquiry.

The repercussions from the *Challenger's* explosion were quickly followed by other vivid catastrophes, and the Journalist in Space program faded away. But when NASA revives it, I hope it won't be limited to astro-journalists. I hope NASA will have the wisdom to send up a crateful of artists and thinkers. True, they're a gamble. They might say something wise or profound, they might have a sense of humor, they might tell the truth, indeed they might tell the deepest truths. The real news isn't about what satellite was launched, or what a systems specialist had for break-fast, or even how the medical experiments are going. The real news is that we live on a planet whose caretakers we are—a sin-gle, fragile, delicately balanced world. From space, Earth appears to have no wars, no boundaries, no political unrest. Its problems are global, as are its spectacles and wonders. That will give us something new to think about, and something old to cherish.

When space flight becomes commonplace, the idea of quest and exploration will change, and setting land or ballooning records may seem quaintly antique. There will be vaster oceans to navigate, with the help of exotic technologies, and concepts like "self-reliance" will have to be redefined. What wonderful fields of deep play await us in space! After the first flashes of novelty wear off, what games will we invent for pure exhilaration? What pinna-cles will we surmount just for fun? What risks will thrill-seekers devise? What creative mischief will artists dream up? Certainly our wordplay will flourish. We will become argot-nauts. Even now people refer to "jettisoning" an old idea or possible "reentry" into the workforce.

Once we imagined our gods patrolling the halls of morning at precisely the altitude astronauts routinely visit. Perched high above the landmarks and affairs of earth, on tiny islands adrift in a dangerous sea, as we abide by laws as old as the universe, our perspective on life will deepen, our sense of gravity will shift. We have planted a workplace in what used to be heaven, and evicted the supernatural beings who lived there. In that breathless sanctuary, what will seem sacred?

CHAPTER FIVE

The Gospel According to This Moment

Earth, isn't this
what you want,
rising up
inside us invisibly once more?
—Rainer Maria Rilke from *Duino Elegies*

. . . people who spend most of their natural lives riding iron bicycles over the rocky roadsteads of this parish get their personalities mixed up with the personalities of their bicycle as a result of the interchanging of the atoms of each of them and you would be surprised at the number of people in these parts who nearly are half people and half bicycles. . . . And you would be flabbergasted at the number of bicycles that are half-human almost half-man, half-partaking of humanity. . . .

—Flann O'Brien, *The Third Policeman*

The baby boomers are entering a more spiritual phase of their lives. Many television shows and national magazines have begun to address this. I don't think it's a coincidence that one friend is writing a screenplay about Elijah appearing in the flesh at a high-society seder, another is writing a novel about the spiritualist Margaret Fox, and I'm writing this book. When people reject organized religion, they often fill that need with deep play of one sort or another.

I have a minister friend whose sermons are wide-ranging and earthy. He came of age in the seventies, and partook of the excesses we all did, espoused atheism, and happily explored the many provinces of sin. In recent years, he underwent a rather public divorce. He is not perfect. Insightful, smart, enthusiastic, inspirational, devoted to his ministry, but not perfect. I imagine his congregation finds that refreshing. When he counsels his parishioners, they know that he has walked in their shoes. And he encourages his congregation to play, because, as he put it in a sermon one day: "In play we see new possibilities, new beginnings, new colors, new avenues, and that's what happens when we play at prayer." To play at something is to fully engage it, "to have a role in something much larger than ourselves, to be part of the script, to be part of the play, to be part of the action." When prayer becomes proper, serious, and somber, he explained, it loses its vitality. Thus he encouraged his parishioners to sing or dance while they prayed, to smile, run, stand on their heads, even laugh while they prayed. "Play when you pray," he urged them. "Do you think God minds? Do you think we look silly and simple in God's eyes?"

We get on fine, even though he understands that I'm an agnostic. His concept of god—the image that forms in his mind when he prays—is not a long-bearded western male. Actually, it's not humanoid at all. He describes himself as an "existential Christian." I'm not sure where he stands on the Resurrection. My belief that Christ was probably a barefoot preacher, faith healer, and political reformer doesn't alarm him. He makes no effort to convert me; I don't debate theology with him. We both believe in the intimate power of a personal faith, whatever that may be, the need for transcendence, the holy interrelatedness of all living things, and the greater glory of wonder. Those are powerful feelings; thus we have much in common. We disagree only in the details, not in the intensity or essential nature of our spirituality. We are both deeply religious people, even though he believes in a supreme being and I do not.

One problem with religion today is that it is mainly nonreligious. We have lost the distinction between a true religious experience and belonging to an organized religion. A religious experience is mystical and wholly subjective; it doesn't include other people. It isn't a set of traditions, laws, dogma, and ruling hierarchies, which leave no room for personal revelations—precisely the sort of moments felt by the founders of the religion. That sense of being stirred by powerful unseen forces, accompanied by a great spiritual awakening, in which life is viewed with fresh eyes, has been replaced, in many cases, by the emotionless, repetitious, and mundane.

Organized religion is an attempt to communicate religious mystery to people who have not experienced it, and most often the task falls to people who haven't experienced it either. What is deemed sacred in organized religion? Not the original revelation, but the robes, the ceremonies, the houses of worship, the scriptures, the ministers or rabbis. The original sacredness disappears in dogma and ritual—physical manifestations—that become holy in and of themselves and are worshiped long after their meaning is lost. Essentially, it is a form of idolatry. Furthermore, people who dare to proclaim themselves mystics or prophets, and declare they are in personal communication with God, are ostracized or worse. It's ironic that religions now repudiate the very kind of people and dramas on which they were founded. As a result, the biggest threat to the religious experience may well come from organized religion itself.

The problem is that core religious experience has nothing to do with formal religion, or for that matter with a supernatural being. Evolution has equipped us with religious instincts, but what we do with that gift makes us distinctively human. We order it, modify it, dress it up, elaborate it even more, translate it, then redefine it and start all over again. We play with the instinct. The basis for all religions is our natural ability to enter altered states of consciousness, in which we feel heightened awareness and a sense of revelation, insight, fearful awe, and harmony. Religion offers a passionate form of deep play, whose peak moments are as subjective as they are intense. People create their own private religions.

By glorifying religion as a special sphere of life, organized religions tend to separate us from the sacredness of the rest of life. Abraham H. Maslow complains that "The experience of the holy, the sacred, the divine, of awe, of creatureliness, of surrender, of mystery, of piety, thanksgiving, gratitude, self-dedication, if they happen at all, tend to be confined to a single day of the week, to happen under one roof only of one kind of structure only, under certain triggering circumstances only, to rest heavily on the presence of certain traditional, powerful, but intrinsically irrelevant, stimuli, e.g., organ music, incense, chanting of a particular kind, certain regalia, and other arbitrary triggers."

The most religious people I know are nontheistic. They experience many transcendent moods, and sometimes even use religious terminology to describe such peak moments. Artists often fall into this category. The familiar makes life more comfortable and less frightening, but it also lulls, which stifles enthusiasm.

Letting go of the familiar requires mental and emotional risk, something which artists thirst for. "Long have you timidly waded holding a plank to the shore," Walt Whitman, in *Leaves of Grass,* urges, "Let your soul stand cool and composed before a million universes." When my writer friend Brenda kayaks with whales—orcas—in the San Juan islands, it may be a creative enterprise that will lead to an essay, but she also feels rapture in what is, essentially, a hallowed experience.

Because our vocabulary offers few ways to describe religious events, except in churchly terms, I do resort to these from time to time. Occasionally readers have pointed out that my books include such words as *sacred, grace, reverence, worship, sanctity,* and *benediction,* and they therefore wonder about my religious beliefs. Sometimes I tease that I belong to a special religious order: Our Sisters of Perpetual Motion. Or perhaps: The Seven-Day Opportunists. The truth is that I belong to no organized religion. I do not require a governing god, and I've seen no evidence of one. If a god exists, fine. If not, it doesn't affect how I feel about the universe. I am simply an Earth Ecstatic. The tenets of this personal religion are few: I believe in the sanctity of life and the perfectibility of people. All life is sacred, life loves life, and we are capable of improving our behavior toward others. As basic as that stance is, for me it is also tonic, deeply spiritual, and complete—it glorifies the lowliest life-form and encompasses worlds. Notice, in describing my beliefs, I used the term Earth *ecstasy,* not *rapture.* To me, ecstasy has a more religious tone, and conveys a sincerity and devotional rigor we don't usually associate with rapture. But am I enraptured by nature? Often.

The need for transcendence, communion, ritual, and revelation is so powerful. If you don't believe in a god, then where do you turn? One of the curious predicaments of our era is having to choose between religion and spirituality. We associate our highest values with religion rather than with our innate personality.

Humans are creatures who strive, who glorify. Science having explained away a need for a supernatural god, we have forgotten that the questions posed by religion are nonetheless bona fide, and that we turn to religions to fill legitimate needs. As Karen Armstrong observes, in *A History of God,*

> One of the reasons why religion seems irrelevant to us today is that many of us no longer have the sense that we are surrounded by the unseen. Our scientific culture educates us to focus our attention on the physical and material world in front of us. This method of looking at the world has achieved great results. One of its consequences, however, is that we have, as it were, edited out the sense of the "spiritual" or the "holy" which pervades the lives of people in more traditional societies at every level and which was once an essential component of our human experience of the world . . .

People have lost spirituality from their lives, a sense of belonging to the pervasive mystery of nature, of being finite in face of the infinite, of minimizing themselves and feeling surrounded by powerful and unseen forces. They've also lost a concern with such higher values as compassion, altruism, forgiveness, and mercy. Dispensing with God does not have to mean dispensing with a sense of the sacred and its attendant values. It's natural for humans to crave spirituality. However, belief in a god or gods is optional and takes many forms around the world, from pantheism to Mormonism. Children learn that being spiritual *must* include a supernatural god, and that not believing in God means not bothering with spiritual values. What a mistake that lesson is. I believe avidly in the separation of church and state. I don't want children forced to worship someone else's god, but I do want them to develop a spiritual nature, and become concerned with higher values. That's how I came to write the following hymn:

School Prayer

In the name of the daybreak
and the eyelids of morning
and the wayfaring moon
and the night when it departs,

I swear I will not dishonor
my soul with hatred,
but offer myself humbly
as a guardian of nature,
as a healer of misery,
as a messenger of wonder,
as an architect of peace.

In the name of the sun and its mirrors
and the day that embraces it
and the cloud veils drawn over it
and the uttermost night
and the male and the female
and the plants bursting with seed
and the crowning seasons
of the firefly and the apple,

I will honor all life
—wherever and in whatever form
it may dwell—on Earth my home,
and in the mansions of the stars.

Religions share many types of rituals and liturgies, but vary widely in details. People are alike enough to be predictable, even boring sometimes, but just different enough to have conflicting versions of each event, upset one's best plans, and keep life engrossingly off-balance. We all indulge in play, but we play differently. Most of us pursue rapture, but define it differently. Some people are satisfied with the easy, reliable rapture of sex or drugs. Others desire the extraordinary. Some need play to be private, others public. Some recoil from the rapture of deep play, whose intensity and near lack of control scares them. One thing we have in common is our need to record those differences. We keep diaries, create art, write letters and books. People who suspect they're going to die soon desperately want others to know something about them. We're driven to leave our stamp, a silhouette of ourselves, on the world. We're fiercely attached to our identity, to our uniqueness, to the miracle that we are living beings. Our hunger for life leads to raw astonishment at being alive, and horror at the certainty that our life will stop. But why should it matter who each of us is, was? And yet that means more than anything. As urgently as we need to sit under the dome of the stars and feel that there is something greater than ourselves, so do we need to exist only as self, to etch our initials on the tree trunk of the century. Life is teeming, anonymous, and disposable; and yet people cling to their individuality to the end.

For example, Timothy Leary, dying of cancer, announced that he had a website and that he intended to commit suicide on the Internet, which he ultimately did. He had migrated from psychedelic psychic space to cyberspace. He continued to have a fairly good sense of humor about life and his own antics. That was always part of his charm. He continued to take chances and stay engaged with life, whereas most people crippled by cancer would have conceded the battle and awaited the finish.

I remember when I published my first book of poetry, *The Planets: A Cosmic Pastoral,* how he wrote to me from jail, using the name "Brown." He later phoned me in the dead of night to tell me that he and his friends were building a spaceship and that I could have one of the seats on board for the trip to Proxima Centauri. Astronomers Carl Sagan and Frank Drake were also invited.

Years later, he came to Cornell to give a talk. Bailey Hall was packed with drunk fraternity boys and other students out for a lark. The crowd was rowdy and came to be entertained by a slightly ridiculous icon of their parents' youth. As unlikely as the duo sounds, Leary had been traveling the country with G. Gordon Liddy, doing stand-up routines at comedy clubs and encouraging the use of hallucinogens. It was a friend of Leary's, chemist Albert Hoffman, who developed LSD in 1943, and took his first hallucinogenic trip while on a bicycle; he dropped acid before leaving work and experienced fantastic imagery and mental babble as he cycled home. But my generation remembers Leary as the guru of the drug culture, and to the generation before mine he was a serious and courageous researcher into chemically altered states of consciousness. As many cultures had already discovered, and Aldous Huxley wrote about famously, hallucinogenic drugs could open the doors of perception so wide that one might enter mystical states. Leary promoted the deep play and religious use of drugs. By the time I was in college, though, rumor had it that Leary had taken too many trips, corroded his brilliant mind, ruined a dazzling career, and become a sad case. But he wasn't yet the clown he would become in the eyes of my students.

A week before his Cornell visit, he had phoned to invite me out to dinner after his talk, and I had accepted, thinking it might make an interesting evening. But when I attended the talk and heard him refer to my "space eroticism" and so on, I began to fear that his plans for me might not be my plans for him. I sensed from the nature of his talk that I might not be able to trust him. He seemed spaced out at times, slightly delusional. I thought he was quite capable of slipping me a drug during dinner, perhaps for my own enlightenment. So I sent a note to him, via one of his hosts, that I had an early meeting the next morning and wouldn't be able to join him after all.

Drugs, sensory deprivation tanks, the no-man's-land of

cyberspace—Leary dived headlong into their mind-expanding waters. He was always searching for transcendence and a replacement for organized religion. I've known other people for whom self-mythologizing, self-fulfilling and defining challenges have served that purpose, too. They strived to become godlike beings they could worship, beings above the confines of family, fidelity, death. They had a pantheon of memories in which they wrestled with the elements or fates and prevailed. Their need to be heroic, and seen as such, kept them on the edge, in the twilight world where heroes become gods.

Leary took his last voyage on April 21, 1997, when a small amount of his ashes was blasted into space aboard a commercial rocket that also contained ashes from *Star Trek*'s creator, Gene Roddenberry, and twenty-three others. Orbiting Earth once every ninety minutes, the rocket will in time fall back and burn during reentry. Roddenberry's widow says that she's keeping some of her husband's ashes—she intends to have her own added to them after death, so that they can be launched into space together.

Whether through laboratory drugs or the biological fizz-out of fatigue, a sense of ordeal often leads to deep play. I once discussed this with my friend Cathy, as we biked exhaustedly through a lakeside nature preserve. At one end of the marsh a dozen skeletal trees stood, struck dumb by lightning. From the park's lookout post, we could see miles across the river of grass. Each time the wind hit the water, it threw a handful of glitter upon it, and the middle of the marsh flared like a Fourth of July crowd holding sparklers. At last we biked back out of the preserve and picked up a lake road, chatting as we always do when we bike, despite sweat, puffing, or the voice-eraser of the wind.

Pulling my water bottle from its cage, I flipped open the dust cap and nursed. No one ever mentions suckling in sports, but what are we to make of the fact that thousands of joggers, football players, cyclists, and other athletes drink from grown-up baby bottles—complete with nipples—as they play? I remembered the ad in the bicycling magazine—the one about biking as a secular religion. I've often had mystical experiences while cycling on my own, often repeated a simple mantra of wind, sun, and trees.

The sky was brilliant blue, the air warming up to ninety degrees, and the lake flashing its polished silver. In some bays, the water was like a single rippling fish—a bass—with a wide stripe of blue across the top, a stripe of silver along its flank, and a pinkish silver close to shore. In others, the lake didn't even look whole, but full of puckers and calms. Water in midlake was blindingly bright, as balls of tightly crinkled foil rolled over the waves. It was a beautiful ride of about twenty-five miles, and more arduous than we'd planned.

Two friends had invited us to the summer ritual of opening up their country cabin, and Cathy and I leaped at the chance, not only to go to a great party in one of the most remarkable of dwellings, but also because we could bike there. The route, they had explained, "is a little hilly." We had driven to their farmhouse, left our car, and biked southwest, following their directions. After the scenic start, we encountered a huge hill, followed by another, followed by yet another. Four miles along, sweating hard and depleted by the ninety-degree heat and high humidity, we started thinking seriously about turning back and driving to the party. But Cathy was sure we could make it, and the tougher the climb the more she seemed to relish the struggle. At the halfway point, atop the sixth or seventh long steep hill, we stopped to rest in the shade of a large oak. I always pack a cell phone on long bike trips. We could ask someone to fetch us. I would not normally have been so worried, but my broken foot still hurt with every step, and I didn't want to damage it again. But Cathy was bristling with resolve.

"I like the ordeal," she confessed. "You don't seem to need that, which is probably a lot healthier."

I laughed as I thought of a life blessed by challenges, some madcap, some bitter, some piercingly emotional, some exhaustingly physical, some calamitous, some agreeably hazardous. "I guess I've gotten it out of my system—pursuing ordeal for its own sake, I mean. On expeditions, and flying, I encountered a lot of ordeals, unexpected ones, scary ones sometimes. There were more chances to prove yourself than you could wish for."

I knew I was slurring over the details, but so much of life's intensity stays wordless. So I let slide all the people and places, the catapults into higher states, the quests, all the moments of grace. But a collage of memories filled my mind, and for a split second I felt again the cleansing fire of ordeal and the austerity high risk requires. "Above the comforts of Base Camp," Jon Krakauer writes in *Into Thin Air,* "the expedition in fact becomes an almost Calvinistic undertaking. . . . I quickly came to understand that climbing Everest was primarily about enduring pain. And in subjecting ourselves to week after week of toil, tedium, and suffering, it struck me that most of us were probably seeking, above all else, something like a state of grace." Spiritual adventure usually involves reaching beyond oneself, using one's body and instincts to their absolute fullest, testing the limits, in an effort to "know and dramatize the richness of physical life," as Michael Murphy puts it. In athletics, but also in some religious rites, pain is invited, even cherished, in the hope that ordeal will magically lead to strength and illumination. A vision quest of one's own devising, whose pain floods the body with such force that it washes part of the self away. Back to *purification, cleansing.* I've used those words myself after such ordeals.

"That's true," she said. "You've done ordeal already."

"To some extent. I still cozy up to a good challenge. But what is it exactly about ordeal that appeals to you?"

She thought for a long moment. "I guess it's being able to have control over ordeals for once, facing ones I set for myself and know I can master. Hell, there are so many ordeals in my life right now I don't feel in control of."

Many men and women I know—especially in middle age—become obsessed with toughening up. It seems to be a common affliction, the sudden need to become inordinately strong, triumphant, fitter even than they were in their twenties, nearly able to leap tall buildings. They create their own boot camp. They sign up for bone-bruising Outward Bound trips. They perfect the body as if it were an amulet that could ward off the Destroyer of Delights. Maybe it's the disquieting proximity of death, maybe it's seeing so many friends growing ill and old that makes us believe that we can master our bodies and thus avoid the perils of illness. Maybe it's because risk and ordeal force one to concentrate on things outside the self: all struggles with identity vanish, and one feels supremely competent in a chaotic world. A seductive illusion. But as Albert Camus understood so well when observing the young men of Algiers, "they have wagered on the flesh, knowing they would lose." Youth is "a land where everything is given to be taken away. In such abundance and profusion, life follows the curve of the great passions, sudden, demanding, generous. It is not meant to be built, but to be burned up."

I remembered one pivotal day last fall. Because my broken foot hadn't healed properly, ten months later I managed to inflame it or reshuffle the bones, and a bone scan foretold my future. I would need a bone graft and a screw installed to secure the "nonunion." Because I was suffering from two leg problems—a broken right foot and an inflamed left knee—my life was full of pain and anxiety. For ten days I did nothing but rest, my feet propped up on a large wedge-shaped pillow. The thought of another spring and summer lost to injury was depressing and for the first few days after the bone-scan results I agonized.

That morning it struck me that I might never be able to go out on expeditions again, or at least not for some while. The bone would knit slowly, if it knit at all. And then there were the other leg and foot problems, which made a constellation of worry. The left foot had a painful neuroma. The left knee hurt where I might have a torn cartilage. On the right foot, across the instep, was an achy pulling that was most likely a stretch of what I learned to call the plantar fascia. I realized that I might need more operations, more convalescence.

I hate the fearful trimming of possibilities that age brings. If you lead a relatively narrow life, I suppose you never notice. But I've always been athletic. First, I was a runner. After knee trouble, I had to change to low-impact aerobics. When that led to injuries, I changed to speed-walking. When that led to injuries, I changed to biking and working out on innovative machines at the health club. Now that some health-club machines have led to muscle strain, I'll focus on biking, swimming, and lifting free weights. But I hate having to limit my choices, hate having doors closed in front of me. I will prevail, of course. I love going to astonishing places to study rare animals, but I also love studying humans and other animals close to home. I suspect my knapsack will carry the same burdens and nourishment regardless of which road I take. It always has. If I can't hike, I will cycle or ride horseback. One way or another, the journey will continue. But it was hard to remember that and to keep my spirits up after four weeks of captivity in a wheelchair, with months of painful rehabilitation in the forecast.

That first evening I wept until I couldn't see through my contact lenses. When a contact-wearer cries, the eyeballs swell, which changes their curvature, and since contact lenses are themselves precisely measured curves, it's like suddenly wearing the wrong correction. Everything looks blurry. On the third day, I began designing the operation as if it were Eisenhower's invasion plan. Taking such comprehensive control of my fate lifted my spirits enormously. This time I would be ready, I thought: the house would be wheelchair accessible; I would hire in-home help for three hours a day; Paul, my spouse, would pick up groceries; all the useful apparatuses would be waiting when I arrived home from the hospital. The time would pass quickly and when it was over I would have a reliable and solid foot again.

Buoyed up by such thoughts, I set off on a tentative bike ride under sunny blue skies. The temperature was in the upper forties, but the sun seemed hotter than in winter. If clouds passed over, I felt chilly, but quite warm in direct sun. Tenth of mile by tenth of mile, I carefully monitored my injured parts. Was there new soreness in the knee? Any extra pain in the broken foot? What would be the turn-back point? Feeling my way along, I continued on to Flat Rock, overjoyed to be out biking in the sunshine once again. The sky never looked bluer, the ice-crusted water never sparkled with more life.

I walked the bike partway up a long steep hill, then mounted up at the top and, staying in first gear, pedaled slowly beside the fallow fields toward the Hawk Woods. Sparkles beside the road caught my eye and I stopped, amazed to see culverts filled with combed-down mustard-colored strands of long grass, over which water gently poured, encrusted by a top layer of ice whose crystals were gigantic and matted together in a thin lattice. They looked like hash brown potatoes carved in crystal.

At Sapsucker Woods, I saw an equally odd and beautiful ice mystery. Walking across a raised wooden walkway, I looked down at the frozen swamp water, in which leaves and twigs were captured and suspended, as if in millefiore paperweights. Across a three-foot stretch of ice, perfect raccoon tracks led to an island of trees and moss. The raccoon was running when it left the

tracks—the feet weren't alternating but galloping, two by two—
and it must have crossed when the ice was slushy enough to re-
ceive footprints. Perhaps on a warm early evening, when the top
layer of ice had begun to thaw. Then a drizzle must have sealed
the prints under more water, night fallen and the swamp frozen
hard. Biking again in the bright sunshine, with natural wonders
abounding, the past and future vanished, thought evaporated,
and I felt whole moments in which I was deciduously happy.

Deep play arises in such moments of intense enjoyment,
focus, control, creativity, timelessness, confidence, volition, lack
of self-awareness (hence transcendence), while doing things intrinsically worthwhile, rewarding for their own sake, following certain rules (they may include the rules of gravity and balance),
on a limited playing field. Deep play requires one's full attention.
It feels cleansing because, when acting and thinking become
one, there is no room left for other thoughts. Problems aren't
shelved—they *don't exist* during deep play. Life's usual choices and
relationships are suspended. The past never happened and the
future won't arise. One is suspended between tick and tock.

To reach deep play sometimes means tackling activities
more complex than one encounters in everyday life (such as
chess), or simpler than one usually encounters (such as sitting still
and watching every movement of a deer). But it doesn't require
death-defying acts of grandeur. One person may enter its thrall
while poring over a stamp collection, another while windsurfing,
yet another while praying. One strategy with depressed, troubled, or addicted people may be to help them find natural highs,
positive forms of play that will appeal to them. As a crisis-line
counselor, I sometimes explored those possibilities with callers.
All people play, whether they realize it or not, and many are capable of deep play, but some fear its apparent loss of control. A
voice inside them warns not to give themselves up to the nonrational, even temporarily, or they might go insane. Or *appear* that

way—then what would the neighbors think? The neighbors would probably be envious, and most of them would have their own uniquely fascinating versions of deep play.

I often find deep play in gardening, cycling, or cross-country skiing. Actually, it can occur in many moments of my day. My temperament is such that I can become easily enchanted by nature's wonders, decoyed away from worry by a fresh adventure, physical or mental. I'm not a reckless thrill-seeker, not easily bored, not *willing to try anything*. However, because of a test I took as part of a National Institutes of Mental Health study (the examiners didn't tell me what the test was studying), I know that although I'm much more open to experience than most people, I'm not alone in this—it's a quality shared by a great many artists, naturalists, and others. Deep play allows one to feel quintessentially alive, heartbeat by heartbeat, in the eternal present. The here-and-now becomes a pop-up storybook, full of surprises, in which everything looms. It returns us to the openness of childhood. It's odd that refreshments often are served during play, since play itself is such a refreshment. Shamans and vatic poets used to teach us such truths, and in these days of misplaced values we need their wisdom more than ever.

CHAPTER SIX

Creating Minds

The creation of something new is not accomplished by the intellect but by the play instinct acting from inner necessity. The creative mind plays with the objects it loves.

—Carl Jung

Great improvisors are like priests. They are thinking only of their god.

—Stéphane Grappelli, jazz violinist

*A*ll language is poetry. Each word is a small story, a thicket of meaning. We ignore the picturesque origins of words when we utter them; conversation would grind to a halt if we visualized flamingos whenever someone referred to a *flight* of stairs. But words are powerful mental tools invented through play. We clarify life's confusing blur with words. We cage flooding emotions with words. We coax elusive memories with words. We educate with words. We don't really know what we think, how we feel, what we want, or even who we are until we struggle "to find the right words." What do those words consist of? Submerged metaphors, images, actions, personalities, jokes. Seeing themselves reflected in one another's eyes, the Romans coined the word *pupil,* which meant "little doll." *Orchids* take their name from the Greek word for testicles. *Pansy* derives from the French word *pensée,* or thought, because the flower seemed to have such a pensive face. *Bless* originally meant to redden with blood, as in sacrifice. Hence "God bless you" literally means "God bathe you in blood."

We inhabit a deeply imagined world that exists alongside the real physical one. Even the crudest utterance, or the simplest, contains the fundamental poetry by which we live. This mind fabric, woven of images and illusions, shields us. In a sense, or rather in all senses, it's a shock absorber. As harsh as life seems to us now, it would feel even worse—hopelessly, irredeemably harsh—if we didn't veil it, order it, relate familiar things, create mental cushions. One of the most surprising facts about us human beings is that we seem to require a poetic version of life. It's not just that some of us enjoy reading or writing poetry, or that many people wax poetic in emotional situations, but that all human beings of all ages in all cultures all over the world automatically tell their story in a poetic way, using the elemental poetry concealed in everyday language to solve problems, communicate desires and needs, even talk to themselves. When people invent new words, they do so playfully, poetically—computers have *viruses,* one can *surf* the Internet, a naive person is *clueless.* In time, people forget the etymology or choose to disregard it. A plumber says he'll use a gasket on a leaky pipe, without considering that the word comes from *garçonette,* the Old French word for a little girl with her hymen intact. We dine at chic restaurants from porcelain dinner plates, without realizing that when smooth, glistening *porcelain* was made in France long ago, someone with a sense of humor thought it looked as smooth as the vulva of a pig, which is indeed what *porcelain* means. When we stand by our scruples we don't think of our feet, but the word comes from the Latin *scrupulus,* a tiny stone that was the smallest unit of weight. Thus a scrupulous person is so sensitive he's irritated by the smallest stone in his shoe. For the most part, we are all unwitting poets.

Just as the world of deep play exists outside of ordinary life, the poetic world of humans exists within—but separate from—ordinary reality. So deep play lives at two removes from the real world (whatever that is), except when we play through the art form we call poetry. Then we stare straight at our inherently poetic version of life, make it even more vigorous and resourceful. Poetry speaks to everyone, but it cries out to people in the throes of vertiginous passions, or people grappling with knotty emotions, or people trying to construe the mysteries of existence. At a stage of life remarkable for its idealism, sensitivity, and emotional turbulence, students tend to respond for all three reasons.

Sometimes when I pass a basketball court I'm transported, thanks to the flying carpet of memory, back to my first real teaching job in the early eighties. At the University of Pittsburgh, I taught various undergraduate writing and literature courses, but I remember most dearly the graduate poets I taught. Not much older than most of them, younger than a few, I found their enthusiasms a tonic. All the elements of their lives breathed with equal intensity. They played as hard as they worked as hard as they loved as hard as they wrote. It was typical of them to discuss Proust in the stands before a hockey game. They also bought poetry, read poetry, wrote poetry in the seams between work and family, met at a bar after class to drink Iron City beer and continue talking about poetry.

After class one evening, we all went to a nearby basketball court so that one of the students could teach us fade-away jump shots, an image he had used beautifully in a poem. Sometimes I

went with them to the Pltt Tavern after class, where we would
continue talking late into the night. With an unselfconscious fer-
vor that amazed me then, and in retrospect still does, they demanded to be well taught. My job was to keep pace with their
needs. I had no choice but to teach them everything I knew, learn
with fresh energy, then teach them even more if I could.

At the end of one semester, in the closing hour of the final
seminar, I asked if there were anything we hadn't talked about
that needed to be addressed. One of the best writers raised his
hand. "How to make love stay," he said simply. For the remaining
hour, that is what we discussed. As I write this, I can see his soul-
ful face. Smart, romantic, unpredictable—he was all poet. Even
now, a dozen years later, I worry about him, hope he survived the
intensity he craved but could not live with. I hope he continued
writing. I see the faces of the others, too, and wonder how they've
fared. Although I could not tell them so at the time, I knew
where some of their emotional travels might lead them. They
were intense young poets. In vital ways, we were similar. I had already endured some of the struggles they were yet to face, and we
shared a common currency—we understood the value of poetry.

When I was a freshman at Boston University, in the late six-
ties, I used to stroll beside the Charles River with a copy of Dylan
Thomas's poems in one pocket and Wallace Stevens's in another. I
was drawn to the sensuous rigor of Thomas and the voluptuous
mind of Stevens. Together they opened the door for me into a
realm of ideas, song, wordplay, idea play, discovery, and passion.
What I loved about Thomas (and still do) is the way his poems
provide a fluid mosaic in which anything can lose its identity in
the identities of other things (because, after all, the world is
mainly a "rumpus of shapes"). By mixing language and category
with a free hand, he seems to know the intricate feel of life as
it might come to a drunk, or a deer, or a devout astronomer

freezing to death at his telescope. His poems throb with an acute physical reality. No poet gives a greater sense of the *feel of life.*

Then he goes even further, to re-create the *process* of life through a whole register of intricate and almost touchable images and events. Working himself into a state of neighborly reverence, he invents metaphors that don't so much combine A and B as trail A and B through a slush of other phenomena. He ardently weds himself to life's sexy, sweaty, chaotic, weepy, prayerful, nostalgic, belligerent, crushing, confused vitality in as many of its forms as he can find, in a frenzy that becomes a homage to creation. In this way, he seems to create a personal physics to match his ideas, so that the language of his best poems echoes the subject matter, and both suggest the behavior deep in our brains, hearts, and cells. He really does nibble the oat in the bread he breaks, intuit the monkey in the newborn baby, see the shroud-maker in the surgeon sewing up after an operation. Sometimes he's cryptic ("Foster the light nor veil the manshaped moon"), sometimes a clear-eyed observer ("the mousing cat stepping shy,/ The puffed birds hopping and hunting"), sometimes lyrically emphatic ("The hand that signed the paper felled a city"). Sometimes he's a maker of schoolboy jokes, sometimes a celebrant seer. But, above all, he can transform the Saturday-afternoon reputation of the planet—a couple of imposing-sounding tropics, its being called a "star," the pyramids, Jesus, Adam, illness, birth, death, sex—into something sacramental. Not neat. Not well-behaved. Not explicit. Not always argued or even structured. But bold, wild, and tenderly voluptuous. How could I resist all that?

Other poets took my fancy, too. I loved the way they illuminated life like a holy text, drawing my attention to how dreams were made, and to the beauty at the heart of the most commonplace dramas and objects. Poetry had a way of lifting a feeling or idea out of its routine so that it could be appreciated with fresh eyes. In "the foul rag-and-bone shop of the heart," as Yeats called it, I knew poetry had everything to teach me about life.

Poetry was all I knew to write at eighteen. Much has happened in my writerly life since then. Although I still write poetry, I've learned to write prose, too, and that has brought its own frustrations and freedoms. In both genres, writing is my form of celebration and prayer, but it's also the way in which I explore the world, sometimes writing about nature, sometimes about human nature. I always try to give myself to whatever I'm writing with as much affectionate curiosity as I can muster, in order to understand a little better what being human is, and what it was like to have once been alive on the planet, how it felt in one's senses, passions, and contemplations. In that sense, I use art as an instrument to unearth shards of truth. Writing is also the avenue that most often leads me to deep play.

These days, I do that more often in prose. But the real source of my creativity continues to be poetry. I've just published a new collection. I love to read books of poetry. My prose often contains what are essentially prose poems. Why does poetry play such an important role in my life? For centuries, poetry was vital to the life of nearly everyone. In the nineteenth century, poets such as Byron and Tennyson were celebrities of Hollywood status. Movies and television may draw more viewers now, but poetry continues to inspire us, reveal us to one another, and teach us important truths about being human.

The reason is simple: poetry reflects the heart and soul of a people. There is nothing like poetry to throw light into the dark corners of existence, and make life's runaway locomotive slow down for a moment so that it can be enjoyed. Science and technology explain much of our world. Psychology tells us more about human behavior; all three succeed by following orderly rules and theories. Poetry offers truths based on intuition, a keen eye, and the tumultuous experiences of the poet. Long ago in India, for example, Urdu poets writing in the verse form known as a *ghazal* were also trying to figure out the universe. A *ghazal* was the technology they used to make sense of their world, and no doubt they felt as sonneteers and composers of villanelles do, that there are truths that can only be learned when you're dancing in chains.

The craft of writing poetry is a monklike occupation, as is a watchmaker's, tilting tiny cogs and wheels into place. It's ironic that poets use words to convey what lies beyond words. But poetry becomes most powerful where language fails. How can we express all the dramas and feelings that are wordless, where language has no purchase? Words are small shapes in the gorgeous chaos of the world. But they *are* shapes, they bring the world to focus, they corral ideas, they hone thoughts, they paint watercolors of perception. Truman Capote's *In Cold Blood* chronicles the drama of two murderers who collaborated on a particularly nasty crime. A criminal psychologist, trying to explain the event, observed that neither one of them would have been capable of the crime, but together they formed a third person who was able to kill. Metaphors, though more benign, work in the same way. The chemical term for what happens is *hypergolic:* you can take two inert substances, put them together, and produce something powerfully different (table salt), even explosive (nitroglycerine). The charm of language is that, though it's human-made, it can on rare occasions capture emotions and sensations that aren't.

The best poems are rich with observational truths. Above all, we ask the poet to teach us a way of seeing, lest one spend a lifetime on this planet without noticing how green light sometimes flares up as the setting sun rolls under.

When Cathy and I were cycling the other day, she mentioned that reading poetry frightened her.

"What if I don't get the real meaning?" she asked. "What if I read 'a ghostly galleon' and think it's referring to a ship, when it's really referring to the lost innocence of America?" I was dumbfounded. Someone had taught her, and many others, that poems work like safes—crack the code and the safe opens to reveal its treasure.

"There are many ways to read a poem," I said. "After all, you don't really know what was going through the poet's mind. Suppose he was having a tempestuous affair with a neighbor, and once when they were alone he told her that her hips were like *a ghostly galleon*. He might then have used the image in a poem he was writing because it fit well, but also as a sly flirtation with his neighbor, whose hips would be secretly commemorated in verse."

"Do poets do that?" she asked, slightly scandalized that noble thoughts might be tinged with the profane.

"I've done it," I admitted with a grin. "I presume other poets do."

I went on to explain, as teachers of the writerly arts do, that poems dance with many veils. Read a poem briskly, and it will speak to you briskly. Delve, and it will give you rich ore to contemplate. Each time you look, a new scintillation may appear, one you missed before.

The apparent subject of a poem isn't always an end in itself. It may really be an opportunity, a way for the poet to reach in and haul up whatever nugget of the human condition is distracting at the moment, something that can't be reached in any other way. It's a kind of catapult into another metaphysical county where one has longer conceptual arms. The poet reminds us that life's seductive habits of thought and sight can be broken at will. We ask the poet to shepherd us telescopically and microscopically through many perspectives, to lead us like a mountain goat through the hidden multidimensionality of almost everything.

We expect the poet to know about a lot of strange things, to baby-sit for us, to help us relocate emotionally, to act as a messenger in affairs of the heart, to provide us with an intellectual calling card, to rehearse death, or map escape routes. As many have pointed out, poetry is a kind of knowing, a way of looking at the ordinary until it becomes special and the exceptional until it becomes commonplace. It both amplifies and reduces experience, paradoxical though that may sound. It can shrink an event teeming with disorder to the rigorous pungency of an epigram. It can elasticize one's perspective until, to use an image of John Donne's, a drop of blood sucked by a single flea accommodates the entire world of two lovers. Few views of life are as panoramic as the one seen through John Milton's cosmological eye. Milton could write "All Hell broke loose" because he knew where (and what) Hell was; he had sent his wife and daughters there often enough, and his vision encompassed it, just as it did the constellations (many of which he introduces into *Paradise Lost*). He could write "Orion rose arm'd" because he'd observed Orion often enough when the arms weren't visible. Poetry, like all imaginative writing, is a kind of attentiveness that permits one both the organized adventure of the nomad and the armchair security of the bank teller. Poetry reminds us of the truths about life and human nature that we knew all along, but forgot somehow because they weren't yet in memorable language. If a poet describes a panther's cage in a certain vivid way, that cage will be as real a fact as the sun.

A poem knows more about human nature than its writer does, because a poem is often a camera, a logbook, an annal, not an interpreter. A poem may know the subtlest elisions of feeling, the earliest signs of some pattern or discord. A book of poems chronicles the poet's many selves, and as such knows more about the poet than the poet does at any given time, including the time when the book is finished and yet another self holds her book of previous selves in her hands. A poem knows a great deal about

our mental habits, and about upheaval and discovery, loneliness
and despair. And it knows the handrails a mind clings to in times
of stress. A poem tells us about the subtleties of mood for which
we have no labels. The voluptuousness of waiting, for instance:
how one's whole body can rock from the heavy pounding of the
heart. It knows extremes of consciousness, knows what the landscape of imagination looks like when the mind is at full throttle,
or beclouded, or cyclone-torn. Most of all, it tells us about our
human need to make treaties. Often a poem is where an emotional or metaphysical truce takes place. Time slow-gaits enough
in the hewing of the poem to make a treaty that will endure, in
print, until the poet disowns it, perhaps in a second treaty in the
form of another poem. There is even a technical term for that: a
palinode. A poem knows about illusion and magic, how to glorify
what is not glorious, how to bankrupt what is. It displays, in its
alchemy of mind, the transmuting of the commonplace into
golden saliences. A poem records emotions and moods that lie
beyond normal language, that can only be patched together and
hinted at metaphorically. It knows about spunk, zealousness, ob-
stinacy, and deliverance. It *accretes* life, which is why different people can read different things into the same poem. It freezes life,
too, yanks a bit out of life's turbulent stream, and holds it up,
squirming, to view, framed by the white margins of the page. Poetry is an act of distillation. It takes contingency samples, is selec-
tive. It telescopes time. It focuses what most often floods past us
in a polite blur.

We read poems partly, I think, because they are an elegant,
persuasive form of reasoning, one that can glorify a human
condition feared to be meaningless, a universe feared to be "an
unloving crock of shit," as philosopher Henry Finch once said
offhandedly. To make physical the mystery is in some sense to domesticate it. We ask the poet to take what surpasses our understanding and force it into the straitjacket of language, to rinse the

incomprehensible as free of telltale ambiguity and absurdity as possible. That's not to say that we don't find nature ambiguous or life absurd, only that the temptation to play and land the mystery like a slippery salmon, to freeze it in vocabularic aspic, is irresistible. Surely this is not far afield from the hunting magic of the cave drawings at Lascaux.

We ask the poet to reassure us by giving us a geometry of living, in which all things add up and cohere, to tell us how things buttress one another, circle round and intermelt. Once the poet has broken life into shards, we ask him to spin around and piece it back together again, making life seem even more fluent than before. Now it is a fluency of particulars instead of a nebulous surging. We ask the poet to compress and abbreviate the chaos, so we don't overload from its waterfall of sensations, all of which we nonetheless somehow wish to take in.

Like mathematicians, composers, and physicists, poets often seem to do their best work when they're young. Once, after a lecture, a woman asked why accomplished scientists and prose writers (such as Loren Eiseley), who turned to poetry late in life, were such poor poets. Is it easier to switch from poetry to prose than from prose to poetry? she wondered. I don't think the genre is what matters, but the time of life. If you read the first book by famous scientists—J. B. S. Haldane, Werner Heisenberg, Francis Crick, Fred Hoyle—you find a mind full of passion and wonder. Those books are thrilling to read because mystery is alive in them. But in later books these same people become obsessed with politics and sociology; their books are still of intellectual interest, but they've lost the sense of marvel. It may be that other scientists, when young, are at the height of their careers for the same reason—not because of their reflexes, eyesight, fresh knowledge, or youthful skills, but because they're at a stage of life when enthusiasm flows freely, a stage when people most often write poetry. "Every child is an artist," Pablo Picasso observed. "The problem is how to remain an artist once he grows up." Those who stay poets all of their lives continue to live in that early state, open and vulnerable and potentially damaging as it can be.

I suppose what most people associate with poetry is soul-searching and fiercely felt emotions. We expect the poet to be a monger of intensity, to pain for us, to reach into the campfire so that we can linger in the woods and watch without burning ourselves or grubbing up our clothes. Then, even if we don't feel the fire, we can see the poet's face illuminated by light, hear her flushed chatter, the blazing wood crackle, and imagine well enough what the fire feels like from our safe remove. Though we can't live at red alert from day to day, we expect the poet to, on our behalf, and to share that intensity with us when we're in the right mood. And if we become frightened or bored, we can simply put the poem back on the shelf. Really, we are asking the poet to live an extravagantly emotional life for us, so we can add her experiences to our own.

Because poets feel what we're afraid to feel, venture where we're reluctant to go, we learn from their journeys without taking the same dramatic risks. We cherish the insights that poets discover: we'd love to relish the moment and feel rampant amazement as the seasons unfold. We yearn to explore the subtleties, paradoxes, and edges of emotions. We long to see the human condition reveal itself with spellbinding clarity. Think of all the lessons to be learned from deep rapture, danger, tumult, romance, intuition. But it's far too exhausting to live like this on a daily basis, so we ask artists to feel and explore on our behalf. Daring to take intellectual and emotional chances, poets live on their senses. In promoting a fight of his, a boxer once said: "I'm in the hurt business." In a different way, poets are, too.

And yet, through their eyes—perhaps because they risk so much—we discover breathtaking views of the human pageant. Borrowing the lens of a poet's sensibility, we see the world in a richer way—more familiar than we thought, and stranger than we knew, a world laced with wonder. Sometimes we need to be taught how and where to seek wonder, but it's always there, waiting, full of mystery and magic. Much of my own duty as a poet is to open those doors of vision, shine light into those dark corners of existence, and search for fountains of innocence.

The poet Heinrich Heine once said: "Life is the best teacher, but the tuition is high." So true. That's why it's important to find time for poetry. Poetry is an education in life. It's also an act of deep play. As Huizinga points out, to call poetry "a playing with words and language is no metaphor: it is the precise and literal truth." Every poem is a game, a ritual dance with words. In the separate world of the art he has created, the artist moves in a waking trance. According to Freud, a lot of play is projection, in which bad motives and feelings may be attributed to others, conflicts may be reenacted in order to master them, and fantasies and wishes may be fulfilled. The same is true of many artworks. Intent on one feature of life, exploring it mentally, developing it in words, pigments, or sounds, an artist follows the rules of the game. Sometimes artists change the game, impose their own rules and disavow everyone else's. Art and play have as their hallmark freedom of choice, and that includes choosing new ways to use familiar materials and ideas. For example, let's look at how artists have taken the bicycle and rendered it into deep play.

So many artists have been inspired by the bicycle it would take a separate book to consider them all. There are dozens of writers alone. Arthur Conan Doyle relied on his beloved bicycle to give him inspiration for his Sherlock Holmes mysteries. "When the spirits are low, when the day appears dark, when work becomes monotonous, when hope hardly seems worth having," he advised, "just mount a bicycle and go out for a spin down the road, without thought on anything but the ride you are taking." William Saroyan's love affair with bicycles began early on and

continued throughout his life. He avowed that "the bicycle is
the noblest invention of mankind," and that he learned style,
rhythm, imagination, timing, how to meet schedules, and the
importance of ritual from riding his bicycle. "Out of rhythm
come many things," he observes in *The Bicycle Rider in Beverly Hills,*
"perhaps all things." Iris Murdoch's romantic novels frequently
include bicycling, because, as she explains in *The Red and the Green*
(1965), "the bicycle is the most civilized conveyance known to
man. Other forms of transport grow daily more nightmarish.
Only the bicycle remains pure in heart." In "My Bike & Other
Friends," Henry Miller writes rapturously about "his eternal
friend," his bicycle, which he could always rely on, "which is
more than I could say about my buddies." In "Taming the Bicycle," Mark Twain explores the sensory delights and general hi-
larity of cycling. "Get a bicycle," he advises readers. "You will not
regret it if you live." There's absurdist Alfred Jarry's outrageous
"The Passion Considered as an Uphill Bicycle Race" (1900), in
which he argues: "A few people have insinuated falsely that Jesus'
machine was a draisienne, an unlikely mount for an uphill race.
According to the old cyclophile hagiographers, St. Bridget, St.
Gregory of Tours, and St. Irene, the cross was equipped with a device which they named *suppedaneum.* There is no need to be a great
scholar to translate this as 'pedal.' " In Samuel Beckett's *Molloy*
(1965), the title character rides a most peculiar bicycle ("To blow
this horn was for me a real pleasure, almost a vice."). Dylan
Thomas wrote a joyous "Me and My Bike" (1965). D. H. Lawrence
describes erotic downhill rides in *Sons and Lovers* (1913). In *Wheels of
Chance: A Bicycling Idyll* (1896), H. G. Wells proclaims: "When I see
an adult on a bicycle, I do not despair for the future of the human
race." To his mind, any ideal future must include bikes, which is
why he promises that "Cycle tracks will abound in Utopia." In *A
Moving Target* (1982), William Golding writes solemnly of a bike
trip as a metaphor for life, complete with beginning and end, and

the hope that one doesn't topple off in the middle. In *The Third Policeman,* Irish novelist Flann O'Brien often celebrates the romance, erotics, and sheer mysticism of cycling. "How can I convey the perfection of my comfort on the bicycle," he writes, "the completeness of my union with her, the sweet responses she gave me at every particle of her frame? I felt that I had known her for many years and that she had known me and that we understood each other utterly." Many other writers have felt their spirits roused by cycling, felt themselves lofted into a state where time stands still. In *Cakes and Ale* (1930), W. Somerset Maugham writes: "Sometimes the road was only a lane, with thick hawthorn hedges, and the green elms overhung it on either side so that when you looked up there was only a strip of blue sky between. And as you rode along in the warm, keen air you had the sensation that the world was standing still and life would last forever. Although you were pedaling with such energy you had a delicious feeling of laziness." Looked at from the right perspective, "Everything is bicycle," as Stephen Crane puts it.

Marcel Duchamp installed a bicycle fork and wheel on a stool to achieve his *Bicycle Wheel* of 1913. Fernand Léger has a wonderful painting, *Les Loisirs,* done in the 1940s, which is a snarl of people, plants, and bicycles. Robert Rauschenberg outlined bicycles in colorful neon in his *Bicycloid* series. Sir Edward Elgar liked to cycle around the Malvern countryside while composing. Choreographers have often included bicycles in their work. Most famously, perhaps, Victoria Chaplin (the daughter of Charles and Anna), her husband Jean BaptisteThierrée, and their son James put on a performance they titled *The Invisible Circus,* in which they became "beings that are half-human and half-bicycle, for bicycle parts grow from their bodies in imaginative configurations, and their movements are charmed by the spin of the wheel." Some might argue that Paul MacCready's pedaling a winged bicycle (named the *Gossamer Albatross*) over the English Channel in 1979 was really a sky art performance, but he claimed to be an environmental crusader wishing to draw attention to cycling's rightful place in modern life.

Whatever artform one chooses, whatever materials and ideas, the creative siege is the same. One always finds rules, always tremendous concentration, entrancement, and exaltation, always the tension of spontaneity caged by restriction, always risk of failure and humiliation, always the drumbeat of rituals, always the willingness to be shaken to the core, always an urgent need to stain the willows with a glance.

The world is drenched with color, and nature is full of spectacles. You would think that would be enough. Yet we are driven to add even more sensations to the world, to make our thoughts and feelings visible through works of art. We create art for many reasons. As a form of praise and celebration. To impose an order on the formless clamor of the world. As a magical intermediary between us and the hostile, unpredictable universe. For religious reasons, in worship. For spiritual reasons, to commune with others. To temporarily stop a world that seems too fast, too random, too chaotic. To help locate ourselves in nature, and give us a sense of home. Art brings pattern, meaning, and perspective to life. We keep trying to sum life up, to frame small parts of it, to break it into eye-gulps, into visual morsels that are easier to digest. The styles of art may differ widely—Dürer's rhinoceros; a Japanese brush painting—but all are concerned with motion, balance, symmetry, color, order, meaning. We also create art as a powerful form of deep play. Even at its most lawless, it has rules, a pattern and logic missing from everyday life, a chance to make believe. It allows each artist to put herself in harmony with the universe, to find a balance, however briefly, in life's hurricane. For me this becomes most personal in poetry, but others relish creative mischief of a different sort.

An especially thrilling creative game involves playing with

phenomena until they yield a revelation—perhaps a detail in plain sight that had been overlooked for millennia. Sometimes it's easy to miss obvious truths, which can lie like diamonds in the roadway and be wholly invisible to multitudes. Then the invisible becomes luminous, perhaps even notorious, until at last it fades into the background again—this time from overfamiliarity—and returns to invisibility by becoming a cliché. One example of that phenomenon is the Magic Eye doors that automatically open for you as you cross a light beam. When I was little, I loved to watch a certain sci-fi show on television. Among its futuristic marvels were automatic doors; they seemed miraculous. Now we stride through them without noticing.

When I read of the just-discovered *Symbion pandora,* a radically new life-form that's pinpoint small, trisexual (it will try anything), and lives on the lips of lobsters, my first thought was: do lobsters *have* lips? But that was quickly followed by a renewed sense of wonder at the quirky fantasia of life on earth. With a mouth like a hairy wheel, and other anatomical oddities, *pandora* is so outlandish that a special phylum was created for it—Cycliophora, of which *pandora* is the sole member.

I must admit, I get a devilish delight when the miraculous appears right under my nose. After all, the marvelous is a weed species. One can glimpse it on one's doorstep. People often ask me where they might go to find adventure. Adventure is not something you must travel to find, I tell them, it's something you take with you. The astonishing can turn up in the leaf clutter, or even at a neighborhood restaurant, in a dingy tank, on the lips of lobsters.

We forget that the world is always more and stranger than we guess. Or can guess. Instead, we search for simple answers, simple laws of nature, in a sleight of mind that makes us uniquely human. Just as we're addicted to rules, home truths, and slogans, we're addicted to certain ways of explaining things. There's bound to be a simple answer to everything, we insist. Maybe not. Maybe complexity frightens us. Maybe we fear becoming as plural as all we survey. Maybe we still tacitly believe that the universe was created for our pleasure, that we pint-sized demigods are its sole audience and goal. Then something like *pandora* turns up, a minute being with a sex life even stranger than our own, a creature that breaks all the rules and gives biologists a jolt.

Because we have swarmed across the world with our curious and agile minds, we sometimes think that nature has been fully explored, but that's far from true. Plants and animals are going extinct at an appalling rate—some estimates are as high as 300 species a day—and many of them are vanishing mysteries. The riches of the natural world are slipping through our fingers before we can even call them by name. Hanging on by a suction cup, and reaching around to vacuum up fallen morsels from a dining lobster's lips, *pandora* reminds us that we share our planet with unseen hordes, and it hints at the uniqueness of our own complex niche.

Recently a Cornell graduate student, strolling through the woods, happened upon a fungus in a curious state of arousal. Odder still, it was sprouting behind the head of a beetle grub. Intrigued, she took it to a laboratory, studied it carefully, asked the right questions, and soon realized that she had made an astounding discovery: a sexual form of *Cordyceps subsessilis,* a mold that produces cyclosporin, an immunosuppressant used to combat organ rejection. We know the tropics contain a rich pharmacopoeia, but for many organisms our backyards are still unexplored, too.

Variety is the pledge that matter makes to living things. Think of a niche and life will fill it, think of a shape and life will explore it, think of a drama and life will stage it. I personally find pampas grass an unlikely configuration of matter, but no stranger than we humans, the lonely bipeds with the giant dreams.

At the heart of the word "discovery" is a boomerang. It liter-

ally means to uncover something that's hidden from view. But
what really happens is a change in the viewer. The familiar offers
a comfort few can resist, and fewer still want to disturb. But as
relatively recent inventions such as the telescope and microscope have taught us, the unknown has many layers. Every truth
has geological strata, and for some truths the opposite may be
equally true (for example, you can't have an orthodoxy without
a heresy). Huizinga argues that science is not play, because play
exists outside of reality, and science is indispensably wedded to
reality. But I think the play element is also strong for some scientists, especially scientists working in speculative fields—such as
exobiology and physics. For example, Thomas Eisner plays better
than most people I know. The secret to his success as an entomologist is his fascination with story and his openness to new
challenges. That he also creates art—he is an accomplished pianist and a photographer whose works hang in museums—adds
another dimension to his knowledge. I've often gone afield with
him, and shared his mischievous work-play. Joyful and completely absorbed, happy to shed the confines of ordinary life for
a while, he takes to the field like an otter to a kelp garden. Once,
in the Florida scrublands, he tossed a moth into a spider's web,
then waited to see what the spider did. When the spider hustled
down her web, spurned the food, and even methodically cut it
out of her web, Tom's curiosity ignited. Spiders relish moths.
Why didn't the spider eat this one? So the picaresque story began.
Before it was finished, he had discovered that the moth was poisonous, that the spider sensed the danger, what plant the moth
ate (when it was a caterpillar) to become poisonous, and what
purpose the poison served. It's always a tale of love and death to
Tom, a tale punctuated by seduction and deceit. Like Sherlock
Holmes, he can't resist the trail of a good mystery.

Many discoveries are happy accidents of play. After a lifetime's search for traces of our ancestors, Mary Leakey made the

most important find of her career because of a dung-tossing game. One day in 1978, in Tanzania, researchers were hurling elephant dung at one another in a playful camp fight when someone fell down and happened to notice markings in the clay that looked like imprints of raindrops and animal tracks. The impressions were 3.7 million years old, and preserved in hardened ash that had eroded over the years. Only partial tracks were visible, so it was difficult to tell what left them. In time, Mary Leakey uncovered a trail of footprints left by three humans—male, female, and child—that led across the volcanic plain. As the footprints clearly showed, the female paused at one point and turned to her left. The child's footprints sometimes dawdled behind those of the adults and sometimes overlapped; the child may have been stepping in its parents' footprints on purpose, a game children still play. Mary Leakey was profoundly moved by possibly our earliest glimpse of human behavior: the female's pausing to turn. "This motion, so intensely human, transcends time," she wrote in *National Geographic.* "A remote ancestor—just as you or I—experienced a moment of doubt." Or of discovery. Perhaps the female heard a relative call, or sensed a dangerous predator. Volcanoes spurted ash onto those plains; she may have been monitoring a threatening plume in the distance. Maybe she was simply enjoying the scenery—the changing stir of sun and shadow, a whiff of newly risen plants, an unusual land animal or bird taking flight—as she strolled happily with her mate and child. We know her life made relentless physical and emotional demands, as ours does, and she felt the basic emotions we do. She would have enjoyed family comforts; she would have feared; she would have played; she would have been curious about the world.

The moment a newborn opens its eyes, discovery begins. I learned this with a laugh one morning in New Mexico, where I worked through the seasons of a large cattle ranch. One day, I delivered a calf. When it lifted up its fluffy head and looked at me, its eyes held the absolute bewilderment of the newly born. A moment before it had enjoyed the even, black nowhere of the womb, and suddenly its world was full of color, movement, and noise. I've never seen anything so shocked to be alive. Discoverers keep some of that initial sense of surprise lifelong, and yearn to behold even more marvels. Trapped in the palatial rut of our senses, we invent mechanical extensions for them, and with each new attachment more of the universe becomes available. Some of the richest moments in people's lives have come from playing with a mental box full of numbers or ideas, rotating it, shaking it, while the hours slip by, until at last the box begins to rattle and a revelation spills out. And then there are those awkward psychological mysteries. I suspect human nature will always be like mercury, a puzzle to grasp. No matter how much of the physical universe we fathom, what makes us quintessentially human eludes us to some degree, because it's impossible for a system to observe itself with much objectivity. When it comes to powerful emotions—love, for instance—each couple rediscovers it, each generation redefines it. Of course, that makes studying human nature all the more sporting.

I rarely dwell on this when I go biking through the country-side each day; I don't worry about the mites that live among my eyelashes either. I have other fish to fry: the local land trust's campaign for acreage, the plight of endangered animals and land-scapes, the fate of the residents of a local psychiatric institution who were kicked out due to recent state cutbacks, not to mention all the normal mayhems of the heart. But a crazy smile comes over my face when I think of *Symbion pandora.* I like knowing the world will never be small enough to exhaust in one lifetime. No matter how hard or where we look, even under our own or a lobster's nose, surprise awaits us. There will always be plenty of nature's secrets waiting to be told. This is one of those tidy, simple-sounding truths I mentioned, the sort of thing humans crave. And I believe it because I got it straight from a lobster's lips.

When discovery rises to the mental whirlwind of deep play, its rituals seem to reverberate with meaning and become ceremonial, holy in their importance. By its nature, all art is ceremonial, which we sometimes forget, except perhaps when we think of the Neolithic cave painters in the *mysterium tremendum* of their task. At their heights, scientific inquiry and art both can teach us a way of seeing and feeling, lest we spend a lifetime on this planet without noticing the unfurling of a dogwood blossom, the gauzy spread of the Milky Way on a star-loaded summer night, or the translucent green of a dragonfly's wings. A ceremony refuses to let things merge, lie low, succumb to habit. It hoists events from their routine, plays with them awhile, and lays them out in the sunshine for us to celebrate and savor.

CHAPTER SEVEN

The Ceremonies
of Innocence

We die containing a richness of lovers and tribes,
tastes we have swallowed, bodies we have plunged
into and swum up as if rivers of wisdom, characters
we have climbed into as if trees, fears we have hidden
in as if caves. I wish for all this to be marked on my
body when I am dead. I believe in such cartography—
to be marked by nature, not just to label ourselves
on a map like the names of rich men and women on
buildings. We are communal histories, communal
books. We are not owned or monogamous in our
taste or experience. All I desired was to walk upon
such an earth that had no maps.

—Michael Ondaatje, *The English Patient*

> The holiest of all holidays are those
> Kept by ourselves in silence and apart,
> The secret anniversaries of the heart . . .
> —Henry Wadsworth Longfellow

$\mathcal{S}$pellbound in small glades where perfect order reigns, people briefly forget the chaos and confusion of the outside world, whose customs no longer matter, whose laws no longer bind. Playground and hallowed ground are the same. Both are temporary worlds inside the everyday world, where special customs reign. Games—especially profound and exacting games—abide by their own rules, and provide their own meaning. "No scepticism is possible where the rules of a game are concerned," Paul Valéry writes, "for the principle underlying them is an unshakable truth."

In the holy arena of deep play, rituals and ceremonies abound. Special conduct must be followed, events must happen in a given order. Even to enter the game may require danger, torture, or cunning. Since the dawn of society, for example, initiation rituals have welcomed adolescents into the magic circle of the tribe. To become part of an elite, a person usually had to be debased and humiliated. For women that often meant infantilizing, for men infantilizing plus feminizing. Pain, ingesting foods that were then vomited, and freeing oneself from female contamination allowed young men to be born again into an all-male world. This still goes on in many tribes, including the extremely tribal US armed forces. There are rituals of passage and aging. Many of those we've kept in our birth, death, and marriage rituals, our religious confirmations, and graduation ceremonies, to name only a few. The military, church, and some clubs practice elaborate rituals of acceptance and tests of devotion. In a sense, all of them are forms of deep play that serve to bind communities together, to reinforce collective value systems.

At first, the rules of these games may not make sense, or they may be difficult to master. But in time, through pious repetition, we learn them by heart. Rituals guide us, help us focus, and free us from the tedium of nonstop analysis. Obsessive-compulsives ritualize to the point of mania, but they're unusual in that. Without rituals we'd find life too exhausting to live. Sometimes the rituals develop a grandeur of their own, and people practice them long after they've forgotten why. Halloween no longer signals the end of the growing season and the rampant decay of autumn. Yet we faithfully costume ourselves as ghouls; and any child can tell you all the rules and regulations of the holiday. Churchgoers may cherish the pageantry of some ceremonies without understanding them. Secret rituals lend a religious tone to many worldly clubs, from the Boy Scouts to the Masons to the Edmund Husserl Canoe Club. Full of complex rituals and exotic ceremonies, sports can become self-enclosed worlds. The ritual world requires seclusion and secrecy, and that blends in well with household routine.

Many quiet rituals have submerged into the sea of everyday life to the point of invisibility—dressing the children for school, going out jogging, pausing for tea and sweets each afternoon, crawling into bed with a glass of warm milk, getting dolled up before an evening out. Rituals of self-care, planned and savored, can rise up like a shimmering oasis at the end of a long dry day. There are real holidays, of course, sprinkled throughout the year. But I prefer personal, everyday rituals. Taking a rambling sort of follow-the-road-wherever-it-leads mystery trip on Sunday afternoons, sharing breakfast and secrets with a good friend by telephone on Saturday mornings. I also like preparing for the change of seasons. For example, that maniacal flurry of tidying and organizing we refer to as "spring cleaning" somehow seems to tug the warm weather a little closer. House magic is what I call it. Akin to hunting magic. A ceremonial activity we hope will conjure spring from the icy dirt, just as in fall, mad bulb-planting seems to keep the rigors of winter at bay. Our need for rituals and ceremonies, for specialness to arise from routine, is so powerful that all couples

and families invent their own private ones to add to those ex-
pected by society.

Home is where the heart is, we say, rubbing the flint of one
abstraction against another. We will gladly navigate through danger, discomfort, and the shoals of despair, if we believe home
awaits us. Wars are often fought to protect a homeland. Think
what Odysseus braved to get back home. "Get-home-itis" is the
most common cause of general aviation crashes. *What makes a house
a home?* is asked by sociology and pop songs alike. A house can be a
simple shelter, but a *home* is the physical manifestation of one's
inner life. Heavily idealized, it includes a foundation, insulation,
and the right tool for every real or imaginary calamity. Hence re-
modeling becomes a mix of obsession and hope, a symbolic revi-
sion of self, a renovation of goals. Small wonder that some of the
most popular shows on television are episodic tales of house re-
pair. The *home* becomes a principality in which certain values are
upheld, certain subjects or words are taboo, an asylum, a sacred
realm full of rituals.

Some rituals are so ancient that few people remember why
the wedding ring goes on the third finger or why the bride wears
white. (The Romans believed a nerve ran from the third finger to
the heart; a white wedding gown was first worn by Anne of
Brittany at her marriage to Louis XII of France, in 1499. Before
that, a woman just wore her best dress, and it was often yellow or
red.) A Catholic friend tells me that, in her girlhood, whenever
she got a mosquito bite, she had to make the sign of the cross on it
with one finger, which she did mainly from superstition. The
bites did heal faster that way, though, and she now thinks it may
be because the motion spread out the toxins. For some Jews,
keeping kosher is an important religious ritual, in which dishes
touched by milk and meat are kept separate. The practice originated in a hot climate as a dietary law whose goal was the health
of the community. When mixed together, milk and meat can

quickly spoil. But one is less likely to heed health advice than religious law, so keeping kosher became a sacrament. In time, the reason for the laws faded and they took on a life of their own.

Some primitive rituals—whose purpose is to fuse friends, relatives, or communities through deep play—continue to feel deeply satisfying: baby showers, where women gather to welcome a forthcoming life into the tribe; birthday parties, when we celebrate a loved one's mere existence on the planet; and holidays that mark the procession of the seasons. Every day of the Celtic year was sacred and required prayers, chants, and rituals to ensure the success of family, livestock, and crops. At the Beltane festival, on the first day of summer, cattle were driven through two fires—to purify their spirit—before being herded to the rich grazing pastures. At night, torch-bearing crofters circled round to bless the crops, and in each home the hearth fire was smothered and then relit from a sacred flame. When seasons change, a ritual always marks the day. Once, at an artists' colony on a Florida estuary, thirty of us gathered to celebrate the summer solstice with song and ritual. In stilted-up cottages connected by raised walkways, we lived along the estuary like a troupe of wild macaques nestled among the green bosoms of the trees, high above a dense forest floor that leprosy-prone armadillos shared with wild pigs, raccoons, foxes, and pine snakes. Spanish moss hung everywhere like scribbles of DNA. Gathering outside my house to celebrate summer solstice, we each wrote a wish on a small pennant of paper, and tossed the chits into the fire, where they burst into flames and danced on hot vapors into the night. Like fireflies, our unspoken hopes flashed toward heaven. Seated at that solstice campfire, I watched each paper wish tremble into flame for a moment and kite higher and higher until it joined the others in a bouquet of sparks, then mingled with the constellations and vanished into night.

Years ago, a friend and I invented Blossom Day, which we

celebrated when her seven-year-old daughter saw the first petals on the dogwood tree outside her window. Then we three "blossom sisters" would gather beside the tree to worship Mother Nature, praise the growing things of the earth, and pledge our loyalty to one another. The ceremony always started with gathering up armfuls of flowers and making a pilgrimage to the official Blossom Tree. There we held hands around the sapling and intoned a few words of thanksgiving. Then we adjourned to the living room to exchange small presents, a symbol of Nature's bounty—pretty stones, fragrant soaps, pots of herbs, perhaps a colorful scarf. After that, the daughter got to style and restyle my long hair. (Once, when I asked her what she wanted to be when she grew up, she had answered "president of the United States . . . and also a hairdresser." I promised her that if she did become president I would positively go to her to have my hair done.) The day usually ended at my house, where we drank peppermint tea and ate pecan sticky buns, and were joined by the guys, whom we dubbed the male auxiliary of the Blossom Sisters: the Sta-men.

Alas, my friend's husband died last year, after a brave fight with cancer, and so instead of Blossom Day, we found ourselves sharing a funeral and many rituals of grief. People gave food and flowers, traded memories, comforted and consoled. As a long-time friend of the family, I knew how sick he had been for nearly two years, but I also knew that only a week before he was upbeat and confident of recovery. True, he had a cold, but otherwise he felt energetic and well. After three bone-marrow transplants—essentially to replace his immune system with his sister's—he seemed to have beaten the cancer. However, chemotherapy had badly weakened his lungs, and that was what ultimately led to his death.

I knew him for twenty-seven years, was friends with two of his three wives, watched three of his five children grow, and enjoyed his fascinating parents. I knew how sick he was and the usual prognosis for his disease, but still his death was a real stunner. For days, I was shaken, paralyzed by shock, and couldn't make sense of his being gone. For so long he had been a constant in the landscape of my life, sometimes close, sometimes distant, but always a presence. He was young (barely sixty-two), and happy with his life, which included fame and fortune and a family he adored. Many of his goals he had achieved. He had acquired power, wealth, access to important people in many walks of life, the adoration of countless fans, and a gift afforded very few: he could do almost anything he wanted to professionally. Yet none of that was enough to save him. His death at the height of his happiness and career slammed us all hard with the same truth: how fragile life is, how mortal we are, how close to death we live every waking second. These are the most obvious of all truths, but by necessity we deny them or we would be too shell-shocked to live. Then something horribly possible happens—the untimely death of a friend—and the invisible becomes obvious for a moment. Dazed, we slip between the figments of time and nothing fits right, not day or night. It takes a long while for the topsy-turvy world to regain its equilibrium.

What happens first is a flood of memories. When I was twenty, I heard Gustav Holst's powerfully melodic *The Planets,* and I thought how sad it was that artists felt the need to deny the reality of the planets, to pretend they were gods and goddesses in order to admire them, to completely ignore their authentic natural beauty. The real planets fascinated me, and I wanted to learn more about them and celebrate them in art. When I entered graduate school, I began writing *The Planets: A Cosmic Pastoral,* a suite of scientifically accurate poems about the planets. At that time, my friend Carl Sagan had published only one book—*Intelligent Life in the Universe*—which he coauthored with I. S. Shklovskii. Because I found a kindred spirit in its pages, I asked him to be the technical advisor on *The Planets,* and he was happy to oblige.

I discovered him to be a shy, modest, easily enthused scientist with a rompy mind and boundless curiosity. He loved to play with ideas, and he had a great capacity for silliness as well as solemnity. As he did with so many students, he opened his lab and library to me, and we had wonderful gabfests. In the early seventies, it was possible to learn everything humans knew about the planets, and with his help I tried to. A little later, he played a vital role on my doctoral committee. Unfortunately, most colleges foolishly demanded (and still do) that students choose between the Humanities and the Sciences, but I always felt that the universe wasn't knowable from any one perspective. I craved the truths of Science and also the truths of the Humanities. Having him on my committee legitimized my interdisciplinary passion, and also made me feel less alone in my own explorations through the world of the arts.

Increasingly, we became friends, and some of my fondest memories are of long ago, flying with him to Cocoa Beach, Florida, for launches, or to the Jet Propulsion Laboratory in Pasadena for flybys—memories of the early days and innocence of the space program, which he promoted with candor and curiosity. During those years, he commissioned two poems from me: an old-fashioned love ode—but to an extraterrestrial—that I titled "Ode to the Alien," and a poem about "Nuclear Winter." That was his quintessential nature, someone who relished seeing things from as many perspectives as possible, and loved asking the question that always leads to deep play: "What would happen if . . . ?" So much happened in his life after that—a landslide of fame, his marriage to Ann, soulmate with whom he collaborated on many projects, two more children, dozens of books, and a television series. But the mind has so many levers. In the sad days after his death I found the years telescoping backward, and some of my warmest memories scurrying to his (and my) early days at university, when he was a badly combed scientist with a world of ideas and I was a fledgling poet.

I hope Blossom Day will be renewed sometime, but now we need the ceremony of mourning, which has bound and nourished people since time immemorial. The essence of ceremony is to give value to something, to raise it up in importance or sacredness. When harsh things happen, rituals help us integrate trauma and loss. They decrease our sense of helplessness. Rituals easily emerge from life's changing seasons and the planet's. There used to be many more rituals in our lives, some of them social, some religious, some superstitious. The real goal of many rituals lies embedded in our need for control over the forces of nature, but also for deep play. At any given moment, all over the planet, people are simultaneously going about their personal daily rituals and also the rituals of their family, community, religion, or country. It has always been that way, since humans first walked the earth. But what a distance we've come, what a distance remains.

Consider one day in the life of Earth. As dawn breaks over a small farming town in Ohio, people begin waking up. Geese clamor to be fed. Light seeps between the slats of a weathered barn, where cows and plow horses shake off the chill of night and wait for familiar humans to appear. In the farmhouse, after staggering sleepily downstairs, a man prepares a pot of fragrant coffee. In a rain forest northeast of Rio, people are also waking up and preparing their breakfast coffee—*cafézinho* they call it—a thick, syrupy drink that they drip through gauze. In Churchill, Canada— where polar bears sometimes meander down the main street— and in the Antarctic's otherworldly outposts, people are all waking up, making breakfast, going about their morning chores. Bird and insect choruses begin singing light operas in the fields

and along the riverbanks. Foggy meadows exhale like great
beasts, and the sun washes over the planet yet again as it has done
two thousand times in recorded history.

On this day, promises will be made, trails will be blazed, art
will be created, and the world's stock markets will rise and fall.
Love will flourish. Hearts will be broken. Children will learn to
speak. New forms of spirited play will be invented. People will
worry and pray. Some will take their first breath, and others their
last. Civilization will go on its green inevitable way as it has for
two millennia.

A day in the life of the earth used to include small gatherings
of kin around crackling fires. That still happens in remote places.
But most humans gather in cities, some of them colossal empires
of metal and stone, where steel mastodons rumble underground,
and crowds spend their days walking from one teeming tower to
another. In the lit Oz of a city hospital, a surgeon will be breaking
open the shrouded box of a woman's chest and reaching a gloved
hand into its snug, lonely muscle.

Our human story began with small ragged bands of hunters,
gatherers, and foragers, desperately trying to survive in a harsh
climate. Through cunning, ingenuity, and cooperation, they
did, and three millennia later—a mere blink in the history of
the cosmos—we are great swarms of people. Poets, astronauts,
sales corps, tamers of cities, people who have not forgotten how
to wish. We began namelessly, and then there were so many of
us that we took the names of our parents, and then there were
so many of us that we took the names of our jobs, and then there
were so many of us that we made lists of our names, and then
there were so many of us that we scrawled our names on
walls and rocks and more ephemeral things, lest our names be
forgotten.

Once we were so few we fit intimately into the life of extended families. As our numbers swelled, you would think we

would feel an even greater sense of belonging, of belonging everywhere to everyone. But there are so many of us, more than we can ever know in a lifetime—or even imagine as individuals— that we often feel just the opposite: as if we belong nowhere to no one. We can move among multitudes, and feel isolated and alone. We live unique, private lives of hope and self-interest. We also live polite, cooperative lives of teamwork and negotiation. When our population was low, that meant cooperating on a hunt or cere- mony or marriage, or perhaps the exchange of goods. We knew the people who owed us, and those to whom we were indebted. We knew our friends and allies on sight—they often revealed talents and tempers in the daily dramas of the community. We knew whom to trust in a crisis, where to go for solace. Today there are so many of us that we forge alliances with people we will never meet, whose names we don't even know—with banks, insurance companies, sprawling corporations, govern- ments, churches, armed forces. We belong to organizations more virtuous and trustworthy than any of their members are as indi- viduals. We belong to our families as we always did, to kith and kin, but we also belong electronically, telephonically, statistically, generationally, anonymously to people far from us.

We are masons, blacksmiths, teachers, lawyers. We have in- vented machines in which we fly, submersibles to patrol the se- cret recesses of the oceans. We have polished the marble of our cities, and also filled them with decay. We have homesteaded the night with electric lights, turning it into a dazzling country. We have learned sin and shame, new words for hate, novel forms of mischief and deep play. We perform towering feats of altruism. Little of it was planned. It simply happened, child by child, loved one by loved one, piece by piece, over the great caravan of human history. In a sense we are a single organism that has swarmed over the whole planet, devouring it. Other animals cannot keep up with us. We may be blessed with roomy imaginations, but we are running out of resources. We have filled the planet until it is bursting with us.

The Amazon is the largest tropical rain forest in the world. It drains one fifth of all the world's fresh water into the sea. Nowhere else is there so much life per square mile. Fifty thousand species of plants and fungi, one fifth of the world's birds, three thousand species of fish (ten times as many as in all the European rivers put together), and millions of species of insects share its tangled layers. The largest snake in the world, the anaconda, and the largest beetle, the dynastes, dwell here along with other giants. From its richness, we have extracted cacao (for chocolate), rubber, quinine, Brazil nuts, chicle (for chewing gum), and an array of heart medicines and anticancer drugs. But tropical rain forests are being destroyed at about 95,000 square miles per year; unless something is done, it will all vanish in the next forty years. That would be a tragedy on many levels, not least because of our need for deep play, sensory pleasure, and an orderly life. What better place to find all three than in the mansions of nature?

CHAPTER EIGHT

The Healing Power of Nature

To have no consciousness of being, like a stone, like a plant; to no longer recall even one's own name; to live for the purpose of living without knowing about it, like the animals, like the plants, no longer with feelings or desires or memories or thoughts, no longer with anything that give sense or value to one's life. There, stretched out on the grass with his hands behind his neck, watching the clouds in the blue sky, dazzling white clouds, puffed up with sun, listening to the wind making a noise like the sea in the grove of chestnut trees, and hearing in the voice of the wind and noise, as from a great distance, the vanity of all things . . .

—Pirandello, "Sing the Epistle" (1911)

Nature loves to hide. It rests by changing.

—Heraclitus

*W*hen summer blows through the willows, I love to ramble in an open field near my house, where Queen Anne's lace flutters like doilies beside purple coneflowers. Although I've never harvested the carrotlike roots of Queen Anne's lace, I have taken essence of coneflower (*Echinacea*) as a tonic to keep colds at bay. Many people practice such homeopathy—swallowing minute amounts of herbs as curatives for an assortment of ills—and in a sense that's what most of us do, psychologically, when we go out into nature. We drink briefly from its miracle waters. We inoculate ourselves against the aridity of a routine, workaday life.

When we spend most of our lives indoors, what becomes of our own wilderness? Safe and dry in our homes, clean and well-lit, at arm's length from the weedy chaos outside, no longer prey to weather and wild, we can lose our inner compass. Nearly three years ago, for instance, when my broken foot left me seriously disabled for two years, I felt lost. For an active person, being so helpless and limited is a nightmare. But the hardest thing about that injury was how it separated me from nature, whose green anthem stirs me, whose moods fascinate me, whose rocks and birds help define my sense of belonging, whose mysteries provide me with rich moments of deep play. Even if I'm feeling low, I can always find solace in nature, a restorative when dealing with pain. Wonder heals through an alchemy of mind. But, exiled from paradise, where could I turn? Once knitted into nature, I felt myself slowly unraveling. Standing upright may be our hallmark and a towering success, but sometimes bone, joint, and spine can't live up to the challenge and act subversively. A house of bones, the Elizabethans called the body. Imprisoned by my need to heal, I craved the outdoors. To heal I needed to rest, lie low, shelve things, restrict myself, be willing to sacrifice pleasure for recovery. But I only managed it with grace when I rented an electric scooter, climbed aboard, and crept out into the sunlight and among the birds and trees for an hour or so each day. I also had friends drive me out into the country. Those doses of sunlight and wildlife were my salvation. Even a small park or yard can be wilderness enough.

For the most part, when we go to psychologists, we don't discuss how divorced we feel from nature, how destructive that can be, or the tonic value of reacquainting ourselves with nature's charms, the charms we fell in love with when we were children, when nature was a kingdom of wonder, play, self-discovery, and freedom. A special loneliness comes from exiling ourselves from nature. But even my saying that will strike many people as a romantic affectation. After all, we are civilized now, we don't play by nature's rules anymore, we control our own destiny, we don't need nature, right? That attitude is so deeply ingrained in our culture that most people take it for granted, assume it's a given, and don't worry about nature when they consider improving the important relationships in their lives. It's a tragic oversight, but I can understand why that attitude is so appealing. Nature is crude and erotic, chaotic and profuse, rampant and zealous, brutal and violent, uncontrollable despite our best efforts, and completely uninhibited. Small wonder the natural world terrifies many people and also embarrasses the prim puritans among us. But most people find nature restorative, cleansing, nourishing in a deeply personal way. To have peak experiences, mystics, prophets, and naturalists have traveled into the wilderness.

Wild is what we call it, a word tottering between fear and praise. Wild ideas are alluring, impulsive, unpredictable, ideas with wings and hooves. Being with wild animals—whether they're squirrels in the backyard, or heavily antlered elk in Yellowstone—reminds us of our own wildness, thrills the animal part of us that loves the feel of sunlight and the succulence of fresh water, is alert to danger and soothed by the familiar sounds of family and herd. It's sad we don't respect the struggles and talents of other animals, but I'm more concerned about the price we pay for that haughtiness. We've evolved to live tribally in a kingdom of neighbors, human neighbors and animal neighbors.

When I'm in a rain forest I caress it with all my senses, and am grateful for the privilege, but I also love temperate forests, scrublands, lake shores, glaciers, even city parks. One doesn't have to leave home to encounter the exotic. Our human habitat encompasses rolling veldts and mown lawns, remote deserts and the greater wilderness of cities—all "natural" ecosystems. Many animals inhabit the small patch of woods in my backyard, for example, from deer, raccoons, skunks, wild turkeys, garter snakes, and other large fauna down to spiders, moths, and swarming insects. The animals all seem busy, feeding themselves and their families, running one urgent errand or another. Their behaviors remind us of our own, their triumphs teach us about the indomitableness of life. We're lucky to be alive at a time when whales still swim in the oceans, and hawks fly through the skies. One day, through our negligence, they may be gone.

There are noble reasons for protecting the environment— one might argue that it's our moral duty, as good citizens of the planet, not to destroy its natural wonders. There are also mercenary reasons—the vanishing rain forests contain pharmaceuticals we might need; the Antarctic holds a vast store of fresh drinking water; thick forests ensure that we'll have oxygen to breathe. But another reason is older and less tangible, a matter of ecopsychology. We need a healthy, thriving, bustling natural world so that *we* can be healthy, so that *we* can feel whole. Our word "whole" comes from the same ancient root as "holy." It was one of the first concepts that human beings needed to express, and it meant the healthy interrelatedness of all things. "Mother Earth," we often call the planet. If Earth *is* our mother, then we have many siblings among the other animals, many rooms in our home. Most of the time, we forget that simple truth, and even pretend we could live outside of nature, that nature doesn't include us.

We really are terribly confused about our relationship with nature. On the one hand, we like to live in houses that are tidy and clean, and if nature should be rude enough to enter—in the form of a bat in the attic, or a mouse in the kitchen, or a cockroach crawling along the skirting boards—we stalk it with the blood-lust of a tabby cat; we resort to chemical warfare. We don't even like dust around us. In fact, we judge people harshly if their house is full of dust and dirt. And yet, on the other hand, we just as obsessively bring nature indoors. We touch a switch and light floods the room. We turn a dial and suddenly it feels like summer or winter. We live in a perpetual breeze or bake of our devising. We buy posters and calendars with photographs of nature. We hang paintings of landscapes on our walls. We scent everything that touches our lives. We fill our houses with flowers and pets. We try hard to remove ourselves from all the dramas and sensations of nature, and yet without them we feel lost and disconnected. So, subconsciously, we bring them right back indoors again. Then we obsessively visit nature—we go swimming, jogging, or cross-country skiing, we take strolls in a park. Confusing, isn't it?

Sometimes it's hard for us collectors of such rarities as paintings, buttons, china, or fossils to understand that we ourselves are rare. We are unique life-forms, not because of our numbers, but because of the unlikeliness of our being here at all, the pace of our evolution, our powerful grip on the whole planet, and the precariousness of our future. We are evolutionary whiz kids who are better able to transform the world than to understand it. Other animals cannot evolve fast enough to cope with us. If we destroy their future, we may lose our own. But because vast herds of humans dwell on the planet, we assume we are invulnerable. Because our cunning has allowed us to harness great rivers, and fly through the sky, and even add our artifacts to the sum of creation, we assume we are omnipotent. Because we have invented an arbitrary way to frame the doings of nature, which we call "time," we assume our species will last forever. But that may not be true.

Off and on over the past few years, I've been working with endangered animals and ecosystems, which has kindled precious moments of deep play. But, as part of the species responsible for their downfall, I also feel an urgent need to witness and celebrate them before they vanish. There are little-known species alive among us right now, which have lived on the planet for millions of years longer than we have, but will perish without our noticing, without our chronicling their ways and habits. I find that thought unbearable.

Although I've had the privilege of traveling the world to behold some fascinating animals and landscapes, one needn't go to the ends of the earth to find an abundance of life, or to feel connected to nature through deep play. I felt rapture recently while riding a bike along a country road just as a red-tailed hawk flew very low overhead, showing me the brown-and-white speckled bloomers of its legs and a bright red tail, through which the sun shone as through stained glass. I often find deep play along country roads, while perched on the pedestal of a bicycle. Making a short pilgrimage by car to an unfamiliar town to bike adds just the right tincture of novelty.

What manner of being is this? I wonder, as I lift the gleaming mountain bike from the car rack. It feels light as bird bones. All-aluminum, it flashes like a supernova, and it has no numbers on the gearshifts. At this level of enlightenment, you're supposed to become one with the bike, intuiting gears in a Zenlike trance of muscle and power. That's a state I've sometimes reached riding horseback, but not with machinery, not flying planes or driving cars or even riding my other bike. When I complain about the lack of numbers to Cathy, she says: "Aren't you the one who said you don't calibrate fun?" A reference to my being a pleasure biker, not a record-setter, mile-counter, speed-demon, or techno-dandy. But we have biked many hundreds of miles over the past year, explored ravishing countrysides and inner landscapes as well, circumnavigated a few lakes, and grown in strength and heart as a result. Few sports allow you to dawdle at speed while you savor and explore the world; thus biking has become an important axis for my life.

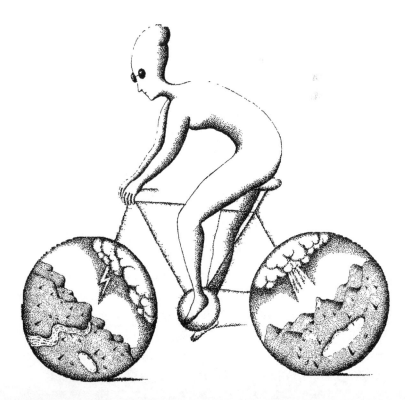

Pure dazzle, this bike is all about light. Sunlight cascades off its flanks. Its mirrors reflect the passing world. Soon we cross a wooden bridge onto a rough, swamp-lined road, and quickly detour into dense fields of goldenrod, wild aster, and tall quaking aspens whose leaves flicker like a thousand silver dollars. A sweet smell of fresh dung mixes with the scent of apples and moss. A wonderful mini-nature preserve, this rail trail leads through farmlands and along waterways. It's one of 700 rail trails groomed by enthusiasts all across the country. Local environmentalists rip up abandoned railways and flatten the beds, adding crushed stone or macadam so that hikers, bikers, and joggers can use protected urban trails as a way out into the countryside. I've ridden on a few, but a recent favorite is a long sinuous trail that skirts Gambier, Ohio. Early one fall morning I followed that trail, while steam rose from the lowland marshes and dewdrops perched on tall blades of grass became small prisms in the abracadabra light of sunrise. The trail went by historic sites and sprawling farms. As I pedaled past one barnyard and main house, I heard a strange honking commotion behind me and turned my head to see a large flock of geese running after me and squawking like mad. *Attack geese!* I said out loud, laughing, and pedaled away from their toothless clamor. I guess they were used to being fed each day by the first human they saw, and on that morning I was it, bike and all.

When a rough trail beckons, I angle hard through grass, mud, and brambles. I love leaving the straight and narrow and hightailing it overland. On my other bike, a hybrid, I'm cautious, avoiding rocks, oil slicks, and ditches. But on a mountain bike I head straight for trouble, pedaling through dips, gravel, splash, and undergrowth with abandon. Halfway up a staggering incline, I shift into a lowdown creep-the-steep gear that makes the uphill just manageable. Easy uphill travel—isn't that what we all crave in biking and long for in life? That, and security on the rough roads. I've never felt so well-grounded: the brakes are sudden and clawlike.

With no number guides, I have to shift aggressively, rocking gears into place, but no matter. I played violin in junior high school—another fretless intrument. Be bold, guess fast, and finesse the rest. When we pause to rest, there's no kickstand for this fellow. Leaning against a tree, casual-like, all flash and dash, it's one cool hombre.

At last we come to the steep unmarked road we've been looking for. I can bike about two-thirds of the way up before getting off to push. Cathy not only bikes all the way, she actually coasts back down to join me and bikes up the last quarter all over again! Her idea of play can be energetic and rompy—we love to banter and play word games as we bike—and we both like exploratory play, even if it's only mousing around the back streets of a village we haven't visited before. But, as I mentioned earlier, Cathy relishes ordeal and likes to play at pushing her body's limits. This is why I've never joined her in her annual August swim across Lake Cayuga. It takes over an hour, and the glacier-carved lake stays bone-chillingly cold all summer. Nor does she wear a wet suit. That wouldn't be sporting. She does swim with a few friends, though, and I'm sure pausing midlake to tread water and laugh together buoys their spirits. Ending up cold and exhausted but triumphant, with a pack of friends in the same fix, is the point of the game. I don't think I'd bike back down a steep hill to bike back up it. But heaven knows I have my own quirky games.

Anyway, I want to stay on my bike as much as possible, because my foot still hurts when I walk, especially at a steep angle. At last we reach the hilltop and are rewarded with a panoramic view of the mountains on either side of the lake, Hammondsport at the end, and two arms of water stretching around us far below. A jamboree of colorful boats speckles its west shore. For a few moments we sit and watch them lining up like chromosomes. A gunshot signals the start of a regatta, and the sailboats lunge forward, maneuvering across the lake a mile or so below us. I love the secret lookout points and all the nooks and crannies of the world that become accessible when you ride a bike. Many others before me have turned to two-wheelers as ideal companions for deep play.

At first, it wasn't the automobile that replaced the horse, but the bicycle. In the 1890s, when the cycling craze swept the nation, hundreds of thousands of horses no longer were needed. Advertisements showed bicycles in the hands of commuters, schoolteachers, courting couples, athletes, circus performers, famous actresses, vacationers, and even Greek gods. Bikes were refined and all the rage; bells and rubber tires were added. They reflected the trends of the day. For instance, the safety bike included netting to keep long skirts out of the spokes. A popular song of the era, "Daisy Bell," celebrated the romance of tandem biking: in one of its verses the swain tells his beloved: "But you'll look sweet upon the seat of a bicycle built for two!" People delighted in inventing novel ways to use bicycles for leisure and business. In Manhattan, aristocrats formed the Michaux Cycle Club, an exclusive cycling academy on upper Broadway, where one could take lessons, ride indoors in winter (accompanied by an orchestra), and participate in such club events as bicycle rodeos, bicycle jousting matches, and Virginia Reel bicycle dances. "Play," Martin Buber writes, "is the exultation of the possible." This pattern of challenge, striving, fulfillment, boredom, greater challenge, greater striving, has inspired extraordinary physical feats and leaps of imagination, driven us to discover our limits, and contributed immeasurably to our success as a species. It's why, when asked how long it took him to create a painting, Picasso answered: "All my life."

So, at one time anyway, bikes were fascinations of the age—the first personal transportation device since the horse. By the turn of the century, there were 2,000 brands of bikes. But cars soon took over as the dangerously adult form of transport, and bikes were relegated to the status of children's toys. When those children grew up, they kept their taste for biking, which triggered memories of innocence and provided a special kind of exuberant freedom. Today bicycles are a $3.5 billion business, and a popular form of adult play.

But they can also be revolutionary. Bicycling brought about social changes that, for centuries, had resisted argument and reason. In Victorian society, women were obliged to wear tight corsets to accentuate their curves, even though such outfits deformed the rib cage, limited action, and caused many women to faint because they couldn't take deep breaths. "Loose" women were the ones who refused to wear corsets, while "tight-laced" women abided by the moral code. High-heeled shoes, weighted skirts, and other restrictive fashions combined to make it nearly impossible for women to exercise. They were imprisoned in silks.

The Rational Dress Society, a British suffragette organization using the bicycle as its symbol, arose in 1888 to protest the deforming fashions of the day. The society demanded that women's undergarments weigh no more than seven pounds, and pointed out that, whereas it was true that women tended to tire quickly when they walked, it wasn't because they were constitutionally weak creatures, but because they were forced to carry heavy weights and wear straitjackets. Comfortably dressed women were seen as dangerous and potentially lewd. Many of them were turned away from posh restaurants and hotels. But in time bloomers (and later "pedal pushers") became all the rage as cycling gear. That allowed women independence, physical mobility, freedom of action, and opportunity to socialize. In an era when politics, business, and education were forbidden to women, who still had to ride horses sidesaddle (rather than have anything unseemly between their legs), bloomers were considered scandalous and politically daring. Riding without a suitable chaperon was also thought immoral, but nonetheless women cyclists gathered at hotels and inns to take bike rides together, and thus the first cycling clubs were born. As John Galsworthy correctly observed in *The Forsyte Saga:*

> Under the bicycle's influence, wholly or in part, have wilted chaperones, long and narrow skirts, tight corsets, hair that would come down, black stockings, thick ankles, large hats, prudery and fear of the dark; under its influence, wholly or in part, have bloomed weekends, strong nerves, strong legs, strong language, knickers, knowledge of make and shape, knowledge of woods and pastures, equality of sex, good digestion and professional occupation—in four words, the emancipation of women.

Freedom of movement led to freedom of thought, and some of history's first women cyclists became political activists who demanded equality and the right to vote. Women of today are indebted to the bicycle for many of the freedoms we take for granted.

As a member of a contemporary cycling club with a quaint name—the WOMBATS (Women's Mountain Bike & Tea Society)—I relish the preparations for a bike ride. Most WOMBATS pack a tea service, and after a hearty stretch of dirt biking, stop for a refined cup of tea. What do biking and a tea ceremony have in common? Both involve graceful motions, ritual, and communion with others. Both focus the mind on the senses and away from the worries of the world. Both appear simple, but contain elaborate elements and may take years to master. Both have as their goal a feeling of tranquility. A recent issue of the *Wombats News* includes this description of a Japanese tea ceremony, by Brother Joseph Keenan of LaSalle University:

The performance of the most informal tea calls for the following equipment: a ceramic tea bowl, a bamboo tea scoop, a bamboo whisk, a small linen cloth about 5 by 12 inches, a silk cloth about 18 inches square, a tea container with about two ounces of green powdered tea (macha), a round tray about 18 inches in diameter, a waste water bowl, a plate with some sweets, an iron teapot, and a small stove. The stove can be a traditional Japanese charcoal stove, or it could even be an electric hot plate. . . .

[The guests] listen to the sound of the boiling water in the tea kettle. . . . This sound has a soothing effect. The host appears at the doorway, bows, and starts bringing things into the room. First the plate of sweets is presented to the guests. Then the tray with the tea equipment is brought in, followed by the waste water bowl. The host sits before the stove and kettle and ritually wipes the tea container and tea scoop with the silk cloth, then cleans the bowl and whisk with the hot water. The guests are invited to eat the sweets as the host begins to put the tea into the bowl. After the host pours hot water over it, the tea is whisked. Finally the tea is served. Each guest drinks with full attention, savoring the warmth and taste of the tea, enjoying the food, being fully present in the peaceful atmosphere created. When the guests are finished eating and drinking, the utensils are cleaned and taken out of the room. A final bow by all brings the event to an end.

"Being fully present in the peaceful atmosphere created" is the unstated goal of much deep play. Cathy and I leave the tea service at home when we set out on bike trips, but we do pack iced tea and such gourmet treats as gingered pear compote, mozzarella and tomato with basil, angel food cake in a strawberry coulis, penne pasta with feta cheese and spinach, and homemade cookies. Not only do we prepare an elaborate but portable picnic, we check and recheck the weather, pack and repack extra clothes, carefully plan a scenic but manageable route. Somewhere between daffy obsession and high spirits, play rituals can take on a life of their own. One of my favorites is wind biking.

One late February Cathy and I went wind biking for the first time. Because the air temperature was a springlike fifty-five degrees, we decided to bike come what may, and what came was a gale, gusting from the south at twenty to thirty miles per hour, with rapid changes in direction. The wind was blowing so hard it had knocked over the cast-iron chairs on the patio! Laughing and joking, we went through our usual pre-bike-ride rituals—preparing a picnic and checking the air in the tires—bundled up in anoraks and set off for an adventure. With the wind at our backs, we *whooshed* along at a dizzying, yachtlike clip. Our wheels spun even when we weren't pedaling. It felt like riding the jet stream. But the moment the road curved, all the addled winds of the world seemed to swivel around us, thrashing, shoving and yielding, thrusting and yanking, then without warning briskly changing direction. Gripping the handlebars hard, we improvised as best we could, and had to lean deep into the wind, biking at an angle to travel forward.

It was like flying an airplane through strong wind shear. Minimum flight speed in squirrelly air is faster than usual, so that when the floor falls out after a towering gust you won't be as likely to stall. Also, a pilot has more control over the plane at higher speeds. I remember one hot and fast landing when I almost threw the airplane onto the runway. Hardly a technique—"chop, stop, and drop," was what we called it—it was soon followed by the mess of taxiing across the airport in high winds. On another occasion, flying around Ohio, I had decided to land at a country airport only to discover on the final approach that my little Cessna was outmuscled by a high crosswind that kept blowing me away from the runway. Three times I missed approaches, circled round and tried again, tacking in at more and more severe angles. Finally I gave up. The crosswind was so strong that it was physically impossible to land my small plane on the runway that day. But I didn't mind; it was fun discovering the airplane's limits.

Years later, wind biking down this sunny road while wrestling with unpredictable and invisible forces, I tried the pilot's trick of speeding up. After all, a bike is also a winglike form traveling through the air. Just as you lose control of an airplane at slow speeds, the slower you go on a bike the wobblier it gets. But it didn't work. In fact, slowing down felt better, gave me more maneuvering time, and the chance to jump off if my center of gravity tumbled. But that never happened. We just called out joyfully from time to time, or whooped and hollered when the rollercoaster ride lurched suddenly. We didn't know from moment to moment if the wind would lunge fast from behind, heave from in front, or pitch us sideways. Sometimes, in microbursts, all three happened within the space of a few seconds. What a bronco ride! A resounding workout, too. We loved it. The last leg home stretched for a mile down a steep hill—but straight into the full slam of the wind. Pedaling hard, we just managed to creep forward in first gear. While the wind whistled through the air vents in our helmets, we shook our heads in amazement and laughed.

That was the first time I wind biked. Now riding the aerial surf is a favorite sport. *Wind cycles* do exist for those who wish their bicycle had wings. Popular on beaches, the wind cycle has a mast and sail, and in a stiff breeze its rear wheel sometimes lifts off the ground. An intrepid New Age traveler once used one to cycle-sail across the Sahara desert. Forget the camels or horses or jeeps or Land Rovers. For serious play in wildest nature, straddle a bike.

Playing in nature rejuvenates the spirit while deepening insight. One can learn there, as Heraclitus did, that "conflict is common to all, and strife is justice, and that all things come into being and pass away through strife." One can achieve a stance that minimizes the finite self in the vast sprawl of the universe, and identifies with unseen forces supreme in power and reality, exalted and mysterious, yet completely nonrational. As many artists have found, nature is an ideal place for creative play. Among the Kwakiutl Indians, a song-maker (also known as "a man of understanding") and a "word-passer" compose music in the woods. Sometimes a novice musician (known as "sitting-close-beside-the-head") joins them. Here is a typical account of an improvisatory song-making circle in the woods, which a Kwakiutl Indian told an ethnologist in 1915:

> The song-maker draws inspiration chiefly from the sounds of running or dropping water, and from the notes of birds. Sitting beside a rill of falling water, he listens intently, catches the music, and hums it to himself, using not words but the vocables *hamamama*. This is his theme. Then he carries the theme further, making variations, and at last he adds a finale which he calls the "tail." After a while he goes to the word-passer, constantly humming the tune, and the word-passer, catching the air, joins in, and then sets a single word to it. This is called "tying the song," so that it may not "drift away" like an unmoored canoe. Then gradually other words are added, until the song is complete. The novice sits a little apart from the master, and if he "finds" a melody, he "carries" it at once to the song-maker, who quickly catches the theme and proceeds to develop it. Many songs are obtained from the robin, some from the waterfowl which whistles before diving, and from other birds. An informant saw a song-maker, after employing various themes, coil a rope and then compose a

song representing it. On a certain occasion when the singers were practicing new songs in the woods, the song-maker lacked one to complete the number, and he asked the others if they had a song. The other composers present said they had none. One of them looked across at a visiting woman song-maker and said to the presiding song-maker, "I will ask her." She heard the phrase, caught the inflection of the rising and falling syllables, and began to sing *hamamama*. As the sound left her lips, those on the opposite side of the circle heard it and at once began to hum, and together they composed the necessary song. This manner of catching a melody is called "scooping it up in the hands."

Karl von Frisch, the zoologist, once described his study of the honeybee (which he adored) as a magic well that replenished itself endlessly. The same is true of any facet of nature. However much water you draw from it, you always find more waiting for you. Lose yourself in its miracle waters, and time will shimmy, the world recede, and a sense of harmony enter your bones. It is spring in North America. The well of nature is full today. Time to go outside and take a drink.

CHAPTER NINE

Deep Space, in Color

In the sun that is young once only,
  Time let me play and be
Golden in the mercy of his means.
                    —Dylan Thomas, "Fern Hill"

But yield who will to their separation,
My object in living is to unite
My avocation and my vocation
As my two eyes make one in sight.
Only where love and need are one,
And the work is play for mortal stakes,
Is the deed ever really done
For Heaven and the future's sakes.
                    —Robert Frost, "Two Tramps
                        in Mud Time"

$\mathcal{D}$eep play unfolds in a magical space beyond the confines of everyday life, a space both physical and imaginary. It has a real place, a locale, where it happens, and that place may be humdrum—a chair, a hospital bed, a laboratory, a meadow, the back of a horse. But it also inhabits a mental space all its own. What ingenious ways we've found for outlining that space—by using color, for instance.

As I enter the Biodiversity Preserve in West Danby, New York, the spring grasses and flowers have begun to bloom. Because I have come for deep play, I open my mind to all sensations, and narrow my thoughts to the idea of color. A male redwing blackbird dives sharply and lands on a cattail at the edge of a pond, displaying his crimson epaulets to frighten off other males. Meanwhile, an iridescent dragonfly barnstorms the shore, darting back and forth like a World War I biplane patrolling its terrain. When another male arrives, the first zooms at the intruder. I follow a plunking-on-a-banjo sound to two large alligatorlike eyes peeking above the water, where a green frog floats, arms outstretched. High above it, a tree swallow flashes a shimmery blue-green back as it swoops low over the water, swings up high, swoops low again, and seems to disappear into its reflection, where pond and cloud meet in the mirrorland of water, meadow, and sky.

A bullfrog leaps among the cattails, making small foghorn blasts and smearing the water painting with ripples. Hundreds of stiff brown velvety cattails have exploded into fuzzy rags the color of sand and caramel. People have been known to use them instead of fleece for insulation. Pulling one apart, I find several needle-sized tunnels, and then the tunnelers—feeding caterpillars whose web binds the fuzz together and keeps it from blowing away. *Tweet, tweet, tweet, I am so sweet!* a warbler calls as it wings past at eye level, flashing brilliant yellow and orange streaks. Wild blue-berry bushes are in flower, covered with tiny white bells. I've brought my own colors into the preserve, as well—a red T-shirt and leggings, white socks, a black-and-white hat, and a red ribbon cinching up my ponytail. I confess, I wore this outfit to play with birds and insects. Hummingbirds are suckers for red, but many other animals respond to color cues, too. For instance, the vigilant, extremely territorial male mourning cloak butterfly will sometimes attack if you wear the colors of a rival male (dark and light) and waggle your fingers.

What we mean by color depends on whom, or what, you're talking to. Our color sense includes violet, blue, green, yellow, orange, and red rays of light. Beyond those lie other to-us-invisible rays. Beyond red lies infrared, a hot ray. Beyond violet lies ultraviolet, which we mainly know by the burns it can leave on skin. Limited to what we rather chauvinistically call the "visible spectrum," we see a unique world other animals miss. On the other hand, we don't see the world that insects and other animals see. Little is as it seems. To my eyes, this meadow is thick with tall grasses and studded with intensely colored wildflowers: purple geraniums, cascading white foamflowers, tawny three-petaled trilliums, daisy fleabane, pearly Solomon's seal, blue Jacob's ladder, goldenrod. Because goldenrod and ragweed bloom at the same time, and goldenrod is showier, people blame it for sneezing fits, but the goldenrod's color and smell offer important clues to its ability to vex. Windblown plants, like ragweed, can afford to be drab and inconspicuous, since they're pollinated by the breeze. Their spiky pollen drifts all over us, scraping nose and eyes. Beautiful, accursed goldenrod, on the other hand, has such a strong smell and color that it's clearly designed to bewitch insects. Even the delicate bladder campions are in bloom: twirly white petals attached to green sacks. When I was little, my mother and I called them snap snaps, and I would pick a flower, grip it by its petal top, make a wish, and tap the sack sharply against my wrist, which made the bladder snap with a loud *pop*!

What playful names we've given flowers. Some are mythic. Iris was goddess of the rainbow. Hyacinth was a handsome Greek prince, whom Apollo loved and Zephyrus killed in a jealous rage; distraught Apollo turned his lover's blood into purple blossoms. Some flowers have descriptive names. Tulip comes from the Persian for turban-shaped. Soapwort produces a fine lather. Monkshood does look like a stem of monks' hoods, although its Latin name, *pardalianches,* literally means "panther strangle," presumably because someone thought it poisonous enough to strangle a panther. Some names hint at their medicinal use, such as snakeroot, for the treatment of snakebite; or scurvy grass, an herb seafarers packed to provide vitamin C. But most flower names are fanciful: love-lies-bleeding, sensitive plant, baby's breath, Dutchman's-breeches, jack-in-the-pulpit, sundrops, to name only a few.

I may occasionally help pollinate a plant by trapping some burrs or spores on my pantleg and carrying them to a distant place. But insects are the diplomatic corps of the meadow, and conning them can be a full-time job for a plant, time well spent. We think of plants as idle, powerless. But their gift for manipulation would put advertisers, lobbyists, and warlords to shame. Color is the most effective tool of their trade. Many flowering plants direct insect pollinators to their most fertile blossoms by changing the colors of individual flowers from one day to the next, thereby allowing the plant to have less than full nectar reservoirs in all its flowers at the same time. Or the plant broadcasts to specific pollinators. For example, in summer, scarlet gilia flowers blaze red to attract hummingbirds; but in the fall the gilia's flowers become more muted to lure hawkmoths, which prefer lighter tones. Of course, this presupposes that insects lead colorful lives.

Continuing along the trail, I pass a bushy autumn olive tree humming with plump bees. About a hundred years ago, scientists debated a simple question: Are we the only organisms that see color? Or is color important to other creatures as well? Do pollinators see colors, and does this help them locate flowers? If I looked through a bee's eyes, everything would slow down. Since bees process images five times faster than humans, a movie of a strolling human would look like a series of still photographs. But what colors do bees see? To find out, scientists trained bees to sip sugar solutions placed in little dishes on pieces of yellow, blue, green, and red paper. If the bees found a reward of honey on a piece of paper, they would fly directly to that color of paper the next time. Soon scientists learned that they could easily train bees to seek yellow, blue, and green. When they tried to train bees to seek red, the bees often made mistakes, sometimes landing on black or very dark gray instead. In other words, they were not seeing red as a color, but as an intensity. Scientists concluded that honeybees must be blind to red. Still, their world shimmers with detail and variety and at least one adventure in color that's only a rumor to us. They see beyond visible light. To a bee's eyes, this meadow is a bustling airport filled with colorful billboards, maps, carefully detailed landing strips. In my mind's eye, I may imagine such wonders, but I cannot see them. The bee and I share the same meadow but we live in different universes.

As the path bends around a large black cherry tree covered in white feather-duster blooms, I spot a lithe figure in the distance wearing brown pants, cream shirt, and a brown hat. Smiling, I call out to him and he waves hugely in reply. Known as "the father of chemical ecology," my friend Thomas Eisner studies the secret life of insects, and I find him in a patch of marsh marigolds.

Evolution offers plenty of clues, but how could he see its private dramas? Tom perfected a special technique for photographing the hidden world of insects and flowers and their strategic use of color. Television cameras are quite sensitive to ultraviolet, which ultimately is filtered out by the screen's glass lens. Tom used a quartz lens—which admits ultraviolet—and through it he began to see the world as insects do. The marsh marigold looks familiar to the naked eye—a golden medallion on a flimsy stem—but through the insect-eye lens its hidden design becomes visible. To the honeybee, this marsh marigold is a purple center with a bright yellow halo and purple petal tips. What's more, the central landing pad—which is full of nectar—throbs with a deep shadowy glow. Like an *X* scrawled on a treasure map, it tells passing pollinators where to dig.

Honeybees are programmed to recognize just such nectar guides. When many varieties of flowers are in bloom, each species of plant needs to be recognizable. Everything is at stake. Unable to travel, a plant must persuade creatures to perform sex for it by carrying its pollen to other marsh marigolds. Squandering its pollen on unrelated flowers would be wasteful, so other marsh marigolds need to be easy to spot. In a heavily blooming meadow, one may find as many as fifty different flowers blooming simultaneously. How do the insects tell them apart? Nectar guides. Just as every shop has a name in paint or neon, every flower advertises itself. Flowers go out of their way to create unique signposts, ones that will make them easy to spot in a crowd, alluring and unforgettable.

A loud hum at my ear makes me flinch, and I turn just in time to see a dazzling ruby-throated hummingbird trying to sip from my crimson hair ribbon. It moves down to my T-shirt, pauses, tries to sip, moves along, tries to sip again, and finally gives up. Flowers offering red blossoms are the favorite dive of hummingbirds, but many people I know have had hummingbirds mistake them for flowers—or try to feed from floral clothes, bright drapery, and even lawn furniture! Red flowers like the poppy are also pollinated by bees and wasps. Not all nectar guides are invisible to us. Some birds and insects are as attracted by certain colors as we are. I remember seeing Amazonian orchids that used colorful blossoms to lure bees and trap them against their sex organs. Other orchids have evolved to mimic the female tachinid fly, so that males, trying to mate, will end up dusted with pollen. Still other orchids mimic the territorial movements of a male centris bee, and need only wait for passing males to take up the fight. Food, sex, or violence will do equally well. Whether plants are drunk from, courted, or fought with, they rub pollen on the visitor.

We may think of color as decorative, not purposeful, not exploitational. But color is mainly trickery, much of it designed by clever plants to waylay a potential pollinator, or used by animals to scare away a predator, or to communicate important (often life-and-death) information. Random evolution has played with the phenomenon of color to an astonishing degree. But humans play with color on purpose, inventing bold and vibrant games. We too use color as feeding guides, to detect ripe fruit, edible plants, and fresh game. We color money with which we buy food. We color advertisements to sell colorful things to make colorful money to buy naturally or artificially colored food. But we also play with color as a sense-stimulating toy, using it for relaxation, beguilement, gimmicks, masquerades, jokes, fraud, recreation, and the many skin games of body decoration.

We even use color as a guide to spiritual nourishment. Religious events almost always include rituals involving sacred colors. When morning dawns at the Mulkteshwar temple in Mapu, India, a priest chants the 1,008 names of Shiva while performing a ritual with brightly colored flowers. The male and female forces of the universe are worshiped with white flowers (symbolizing semen) and red flowers (symbolizing menstrual blood). Then marigold petals are offered as a symbol of purification. Before the ritual is complete, there is much lighting of lamps, because, according to Hindu philosophy, colors emerged from a single flame. Western astrophysicists would probably agree.

On the same morning, along the banks of the Ganges, bathers pause at the Golden Temple to have their foreheads touched with color—yellow sandalwood as a symbol of Shiva. At the river bank, a priest wearing yellow robes over his red-stained skin is celebrating Holi, the festival of spring, whose patron god is Krishna. In a final stage of complexly erotic ceremonies, men will tease women by singing lascivious songs and sprinkling them with colored water, and an exuberant crowd will toss clouds of red powder into the air, showering everyone with crimson.

In nature, flashy dress usually signifies danger. Arrow-poison frogs announce in screaming colors: *Don't touch!* So do monarch butterflies, heart-stoppingly beautiful with their digitalislike poison. Banded bumblebees warn of stingers, diamondbacked rattlers of fangs. "Dangerous if attacked or eaten," their colors proclaim. Even plants use color to communicate danger. As Dr. Michael Kasperbauer of the USDA Coastal Plains Research Center has discovered, when plants are exposed to far-red, a color beyond human vision, they react as if they were threatened by rivals, spiraling high and boosting the chlorophyll and protein in their leaves. Fearful tomato plants grow taller faster and fruit earlier than their competitors. Kasperbauer found equally intriguing results when he exposed cotton and turnip plants to blue. Ambitious growers can buy a variety of colored mulches, beginning with far-red.

Birds do it, bees do it, even little fleas do it—use color to attract a mate. Female spotted turtles, hamadryas baboons, birds of paradise, and countless other animals signal fertility with color. Femme-fatale lightning bugs cleverly decipher the semaphore of their rivals in order to lure and steal other females' mates. I suppose in the world of fireflies they would be known not as scarlet but "chartreuse" women. Indeed, animals respond so zealously to color that they sometimes overlook the obvious. When I was in the Antarctic, I found myself in a large colony of black-and-yellow king penguins. I happened to be wearing a bright yellow sweatsuit and I wore my black hair long. I also happened to know the female king penguin's courtship dance. When I knelt and swung my head like a female penguin doing a mating display, a male immediately left the colony, waddled over at speed, and took a good long look at me, pacing anxiously back and forth, looking, looking, before he decided I might not be his type. I was all the right colors to trigger his lust—well, *almost* the right colors and moving in *almost* the right way.

When I hear the distant trills of a rehearsing opera singer, I smile: somewhere, barely visible, gray tree frogs are advertising for mates. It's fascinating how animals use color for camouflage. A green damselfly, whose transparent wings help it disappear among last year's Queen Anne's lace, becomes visible only when it twitters into flight at my knee. Perching, it disappears; fluttering, it reappears. Thousands of goldenrods seem frothing at the mouth, because they're full of spittle bugs, tiny critters that produce a façade of white spume to hide beneath while they suck the plant leaves. The optical illusion known as countershading works for many animals, including penguins, which are black on the top so that leopard seals and other predators won't see them when looking down through ocean depths; and white on their bellies so that the same predators, looking up, will confuse them with clouds and sky. But there are even subtler disguises.

"Can you see the caterpillar on this leaf?" Tom asks, pointing at what looks like a familiar jumble of leaves.

Peering, squinting, stepping back, bending low, I look hard. Something twitches and I point to it.

"The caterpillar disguises itself in petals," he explains. "Put it on a plant and it gives immediate priority to dressing itself up. It sews them onto its back, where it has special spines."

A hooded warbler flies into a tall ash tree, buzz-calling what sounds like *I am lazy. I am lazy.* I can't help but wonder how many times Tom saw his three daughters play dress-up when they were small, or how many Halloween costumes he and his wife Maria helped them create. Over the years, Maria has mastered the scanning electron microscope, and produced astonishing images of minutely distant worlds.

"That sounds like a lot of work. What does it sew with?"

"Threads of silk manufactured from special glands. It reaches over the petal from the spine, puts a little silk around here, and *voilà!* we have a perfectly costumed caterpillar. Obviously a very effective means of defense."

"Caterpillars sewing costumes?" It looks like a Chinese dragon in a New Year's Day parade. "Crafty little thing."

"Isn't it amazingly skillful?"

A nearby stone glows in a jacket of red lichen. It would make a beautiful dye for a Chinese dragon costume. Indeed, many of the preserve's plants and minerals would produce delicate or indelible stains. But these 270 acres of forest, wetlands, meadows, and ponds have been set aside as the first Biodiversity Preserve in a temperate climate, and may not be exploited, except benignly, in a way so discreet as to be thrilling. We think of the Amazon as a pantry of undiscovered marvels, but it occurred to Tom that many unknown chemicals lurk in temperate forests. Thus he helped establish this preserve for chemical prospecting. It's open to hikers, cross-country skiers, and birders, of course, but also is hospitable to people searching for new drugs, organic pesticides, and other pharmaceuticals. Beautiful as the red lichen may be, gathering enough for a dye would be taboo. If I lived in Harris, Scotland, on the other hand, I'd find dyers collecting bushels of the local brownish-orange lichen, which gives Harris tweed its distinctive color and odor. Fashionably respectable, Harris tweed qualifies both as display and social camouflage. But I doubt many of its devotees know they're clad in lichen. It's hard enough for humans to dress themselves ingeniously. How on earth does this caterpillar get it right?

"Well, suppose it takes the correct petals," I ask Tom after a moment, "but doesn't always put them on in the right way?"

His face lights up. "In fact it *does* make mistakes and then it ends up being very conspicuous and that's a real hazard, because the caterpillars are hunted by little wasps that can see in ultraviolet."

"How will the costume drama of this caterpillar end?" I ask. "Will it master its disguise?"

"We're dealing with a remarkable situation," Tom says excitedly, "in which we can watch evolution in action right now. The caterpillar is doing a good job, but it's not perfectly camouflaged yet. So any mistake could prove fatal." As dire as that sounds, Tom is clearly delighted to watch the trials of nature unfold and try to guess what-will-be. Meanwhile, the caterpillar juggles the petals, searching for a masquerade that will succeed.

If the caterpillar's sewing tricks seem strange, one need only remember that human costume and play have produced some mighty odd camouflage fashions, including my personal favorite: the floor-length gowns worn at Versailles during the reign of Louis XIV. In that era, clothes were so infested with fleas that master dyers created a special color for the gowns to make crawling insects a little less obvious. They called the hue "puce," which is French for flea. Privileged and jaded decadents in Marie Antoinette's court also wore gowns in such camouflage colors as "dead flea," "flea shit," and "baby's vomit." At least they had a sense of humor about their infestation. Nobility being what it is, puce and other flea tones soon became all the rage in France.

Like other animals, we use color to communicate all sorts of information, even mood. An emotional octopus changes color. We do the same. When we're embarrassed we blush. Like the hummingbird and the tomato, we respond passionately to red, a blood color that excites our senses, sometimes into fright, but most often into arousal. Hence the cliché of the seductive "scarlet" woman in a red dress, which has some basis in fact. When a man sees bright red, his pituitary gland tells his adrenal gland to secrete more adrenaline and get his body ready for action. It's no surprise that Marlboro cigarettes, Coca-Cola, Campbell's soups, Budweiser beer, Colgate toothpaste, and countless other products rely on red in their advertisements and packaging to entice consumers.

Of course, we also use color to express status or power, and many potentates have amused themselves by conquering a favorite hue. According to Roman law, for example, only emperors could wear Tyrian purple, a sumptuous shade that Pliny the Elder described as "the color of congealed blood, blackish at first, but gleaming when held up to the light." It was obtained by crushing murex, a Mediterranean shellfish, and illegal purveyors of the purple dye could be put to death. Montezuma and other Aztec emperors claimed the right to wear royal red, which meant imposing on their subjects a special tax to be paid in cochineal insects, from which the vibrant dye came. When the Spanish arrived, they conquered the cochineal trade, and in 1587 alone sent sixty-five tons of cochineal to Spain. Their monopoly of royal red finally ended when a French naturalist smuggled cochineal insects and their host plant, the prickly pear cactus, to France.

We're so addicted to color that some cultures have found novel games to play with it, including the telling of time. In eighteenth-century France, the "white hour" was the hour before dinner when the gentry powdered their wigs, the "lavender hour" the delicate one just before sunset. We even believe our gods prefer special colors. Each year in spring, at a Buddhist temple in Nara, the ancient capital of Japan, monks make 500 paper camellias in red and white—the most auspicious colors—with which to celebrate the traditional ceremony of Water Drawing. Throughout the world, henna's lustrous red dye is favored as a hair and body stain. Using the body as a canvas, artists create intricate henna-red designs, some according to traditional patterns, but others improvisatory and modern. In Delhi, women attending a wedding will decorate their hands with henna paste, which they leave on for an hour, softening the color with coconut oil, and applying lime juice (to darken the tint), finally rinsing their richly stained hands with oil. In Luxor, on the eve of their wedding, a bride and groom will enjoy a "henna night" party. Powdered henna is diluted with water and sugar (to guarantee a sweet life), and baked into a cake, which dancers balance on their heads. Finally, the henna cake is used to dye the hands and feet. Beautiful as henna may be, in Islamic tradition it also grants purification; thus henna staining is a vital part of weddings, baby showers, and burials. In ancient Egypt, mummification rites included henna, and for centuries color merchants offered European painters (including Rembrandt) a pigment known as "mummy," a potent brown made from the crushed remains of the henna-imbued mummies.

A blue jay takes flight, leaving a deep-blue feather on the ground behind it. Picking up the feather, I turn it every which way, and to me it still looks blue. When I crush the feather, it suddenly becomes a dull grayish brown. Color doesn't appear in the world, but in the mind. Blue jays only appear blue because of the way light strikes cells lying along the feathers. The same is true of the Morpho butterfly's luminous blue wings, where millions of intricately ridged scales produce the illusion of blue. "The precision is extraordinary, very sharply tuned to a particular wavelength of light"—Tom has glimpsed them through a scanning electron microscope. When Nissan Motor Company realized why Morphos look blue, it created a fluorescent blue car finish based on the same law of structural (rather than pigmented) color. Much of what we call color is really architecture on a microscopic scale. The color of a polar bear's fur is not white but transparent. Air bubbles inside the fur catch the light in a way that we perceive as "white." Apples are not red. The sky is not blue. Actually an apple is everything *but* red, the sky is everything *but* blue. The red rays, bouncing off the apple, are rejected by it; seeing that happen, we think "red." Overhead, the clear sky is not blue but slippery. Blue light rays skid off the molecules of air, and so the sky seems to be full of "blue." Even blue eyes are not inherently blue, not stained blue like the fabric of a sari. Eyes appear blue for the same reason the sky does—when light enters blue eyes, short blue rays scatter as they jump off tiny, nonpigmented particles. What we see are scattered rays: eyes shining blue.

All around me, there are so many shades of green. Why do there need to be *so many* greens? Although it didn't evolve for our pleasure, green seems to be a color we respond to deeply. Think of *playing*, and most likely you'll picture a field of green grass and trees, in memory of backyard play, school playgrounds, or team sports at a stadium. According to Swiss researcher Max Luscher, whose color test is widely used in Europe to screen job applicants, people who prefer green tend to be firm, constant, and resistant to change. Recalling the faces of environmentalist friends who prefer the color green, indeed are known as "Greens," I wonder if they tend to be "firm, constant, resistant to change." They have those, and many other qualities. However, they live by paradox, as so many of us do. Wishing to keep nature intact, they are resistant to change. But the essence of nature *is* change.

That change is usually signaled and revealed by color. Example: the changing colors of a monarch butterfly's Fabergé-like chrysalis, and, perhaps most famously, the glory of turning leaves in the fall. In a few months, the Preserve will teem with vibrantly colored fall leaves. Although they will appear to be adding color, it is really a form of subtraction. The colors were there all along, but hidden by the chlorophyll-rich greens of summer. When the trees stop producing chlorophyll and pare down for winter, the brilliant reds and oranges—that were always there but masked by green—become visible for the first time all year. Once again we discover how much of color is hidden from human view. But illusion has always been at the heart of color, which becomes clear if we trace the word "color" to its source in the Indo-European root *kel-* which meant "hide" (and is the origin of such words as *apocalypse, clandestine, conceal, occult*).

In the lavender hour of twilight, a glorious sunset begins with a slow caravan of red, orange, and yellow gushing behind the forest of aspen and pine. At last it builds to a swirling tumult of scarlet, fuchsia, and deepest purple. All over the world people witness and celebrate this daily marvel, as sunlight traveling through the lens of the atmosphere bends into intense, ambiguous colors. How we love to play with color. I picture the neon lights of Hong Kong; the carnival costumes in Rio de Janeiro; New Guinea warriors in paint, masks, and headdresses; Spanish flamenco dancers; a Van Gogh being auctioned; Hopi kachina dancers. Our passion for color connects us intimately to people everywhere, but also to plants and animals. We are all of us bamboozled by its trickery, exalted by its richness, and enslaved by its messages. Craving color like a drug, we will rise at dawn, or trek long distances to scenic lookout points, just to drink color from the fountains of the sun.

CHAPTER TEN

The Night
of the Comet

Some things turn me on as if I'd swallowed a neon
sign.

—Smoke Blanchard, high-altitude climber

I grow less and less afraid of the presence of skeptics
and of their opinions. Little by little, I am escaping
from their grasp, on the understanding that they
provide me with food for my ohs! and ahs!, which
don't make a great noise but come from a long
way down, and on condition also that they furnish
me with my daily subject of amazement. A lack of
money, if it be relative, and a lack of comfort can
be endured if one is sustained by pride. But not the
need to be astounded. Astound me, try your hardest.
These last flashes of astonishment are what I cannot
live without.

—Colette, *Earthly Paradise*

*W*hatever the future may hold, we should expect a dramatic change in how we regard the body and play with its mysteries. Once it was revered as an astonishing combination of contraption, temple, and resort. Doctors remembering their med-school days of dissecting cadavers often report a gradual ascent from a practical, bone-and-gristle, up-to-their-elbows-in-stench attitude to one of wonderment and deep respect. What will happen when intimacy no longer requires physical contact? When the senses are denied? Recently, a dead woman was sliced up, scanned by an MRI machine, digitalized, and fed into the Internet so that web warriors and net surfers could download her and learn the mysteries of the human body. This is all part of the Visible Human Project, a momentous futuristic feat. By far, it is the strangest of all computer games. I'm concerned about how unknowable this woman continues to be, and what will always be lacking from any *Gray's Anatomy*, even a cyberspace one.

In similar sense, the Barbie doll was also a virtual woman, a cartoon version. This new cell-by-cell female is more scientifically accurate, but just as much a cipher. She's closer to a three-dimensional poster than to a human. Although she's a very useful cadaver, students can dissect her without the usual unpleasantness—all the devastating smells of death and formaldehyde that are nearly impossible to wash off one's hands—and that makes studying her both thrilling and dangerously bland.

Isn't this what Marshall McLuhan was warning us about ages ago? There will come a time, he predicted, when we'll happily eat the menu instead of the food. With the Virtual Woman, a new era begins in which we study the picture of a woman as though she were real, not another flat abstraction, another kind of poster tacked up on the inside of a locker door.

I understand the hunger, tapped by the movie *Fantastic Voyage*,

I too want to roam around the islet of Langerhans, study the heart valves, pause at a synaptic junction. We long to know who we are, to understand how we exist. It is a dignified and noble hunger. Of course we want a reliable cartography of the human body. When I was a child, we had see-through plastic people (minus genitals) called the Visible Man and the Visible Woman. The danger is that, in our eagerness and sloth, we may confuse the menu with the meal, mistake the cartoon woman for the real McCoy, tend to disregard the awkward and messy emotional life this woman lived. I know her life was awkward and messy, because all lives are. That's what makes them so fascinating, ultimately unknowable, and quirky enough to digitalize a dream.

The Virtual Man and Virtual Woman are odd bedfellows on the Noah's ark of computerland. Ironically, they are electrical phantoms, just as the real man and woman were, ghostly portraits of who they were at the moment when they ceased to exist. Only now they exist forever. Empty vessels. Microscopic postcards. Hard-time felons make an unlikely Adam and Eve. Maybe they will just be a chapter from the brave new Garden of Eden, soon to be followed by whole libraries of people for us to undress and ogle. It says a lot about our quest for self-understanding, and also about our retreat from the mucky, smelly, hands-on experience of our senses. Sanitize horror and it loses its punch. Hobble all the senses except the visual, and you produce curiously deprived voyeurs. Death *should* be disturbing. It should affect us viscerally, not just fascinate us but also fill us with lament and compassion. Should it provide a playground for cyberspace anatomists and casual Internet browsers alike? Does it matter what games they devise to play with the digitalized remains of people? As more bodies become available, we will have many questions to consider. Among them will be what sort of doctors we hope to produce.

Dr. Lewis Thomas, a poetic essayist and one of our brightest

spirits—someone in whose hands civilization would be safe—
wrote poetry, and believed that doctors need to be well-rounded
humanists. I remember visiting him one day in his office on the
top floor of the Sloan-Kettering Cancer Institute, of which he was
director. Eating lunch from hospital trays, we sat and discussed
contemporary poetry, among other things. I had brought him an
offprint of Paul West's colorful essay about migraines I thought
might interest him, and it did. Part of Lewis Thomas's great
charm was that his wonder nerves were close to the surface. He
took one look at the offprint, flashed a youthful grin, and exclaimed, "Hot dog!"

Thomas used to advise medical students to temper the aus-
tere mechanics of medicine with compassion, tenderness, and
wisdom. Although he hated the idea of treating patients, or any
people for that matter, as mere objects, he respected them in the
round, and devoted his life—both as a writer and as a doctor—to
healing the whole person, ailing body and murmurous soul. I can
only imagine what he would have made of finding a virtual
woman on his computer, her organs succinct and detachable. I
think he might have downloaded her heart, and noticed that it
looks like a haiku.

Something else that would have given him pause is the computer program EMI (pronounced "Emmy"). Designed by composer David Cope to help during dry periods, EMI can generate
exquisite new Mozart symphonies, symphonies that experts can't
distinguish as fakes. Indeed, running on a standard Macintosh
computer, EMI can also turn out plausible new works by Bach,
Beethoven, Brahms, Chopin, and other greats. This wouldn't be
so threatening if her compositions were lifeless forgeries, techni-
cally right yet unsubtle; but she can compose new works by
Mozart more ingeniously, more touchingly, than humans can.
We identify the hard work of art with uniquely talented souls,
who create from raw need in an ecstasy of deep play. What does it

mean if an emotionless, wisdomless, thoughtless, passionless, completely painfree computer program can compose breathtaking works of expressive music? When Douglas Hofstadter, a cognitive scientist and pianist, first played EMI's new "Chopin" mazurka, he was stunned. "EMI has no model whatsoever of life experiences, has no sense of itself, has no sense of Chopin, has never heard a note of music, has no trace in it of the place where I think music comes from. Not a trace," he exclaimed. "I'm comparing that with an entire human soul, one forged by the struggles and travails of life, and all the experiences that create emotion: turmoil, excitement, hope, despair, resignation, everything you want to think of that goes into building a character." Yet EMI's fine mazurka sounds like it truly belongs in Chopin's opus. A virtual composer of EMI's skill is worrisome. Can great music be written without the heart and soul of a genius? "If that's the case—and I'm not saying it is—then I've been fooled by music all my life," Hofstadter laments. "I've been sucked in by a vast illusion. And that would be for me an absolute tragedy, because my entire life I've been moved by music. I've always felt I've been coming in contact with the absolute essence of humanity." I'm sure Lewis Thomas—who wrote lovingly of how Gustav Mahler's music moved him—would agree. Virtual humans, virtual artists. If composers who aren't capable of great works can create computer programs that are—where does the creative act lie? At a party years ago, British astronomer Sir Fred Hoyle was musing about what he would like to be, were he not an astronomer. He said he would want to be Bach, so that he could compose even more Bachian music, which he assumed required that he *become* that uniquely talented human being. On the most basic level, a well-tutored computer can play with patterns, intervals, and motifs—just as evolution can. But there is a vast difference between basic play and deep play, between fiddling with patterns and inspired, rapturous acts of creation. Or so we thought. Now what? Do we redefine creativity? Do we move the yardstick so as to exclude nonhumans? Do we place computer artists in the same category as elephant, chimpanzee, or dolphin painters? Or do we recognize the human tutelage in some way? Given the new sacred playgrounds of cyberspace, where on earth will the play spirit lead us in the new millennium? Perhaps all the way to heaven.

Many forms of play can sweep one along on gradual waves of laughter and ingenuity, while others—religious mysticism, sports, composing music, adventuring—can swiftly become elevating, of cosmic importance, deadly serious, and thrillingly addictive. "At the peak of a tremendous and victorious effort," Russian weight-lifter Yuri Vlasov told a reporter, "while the blood is pounding in your head, all suddenly becomes quiet within you. At that moment you have the conviction that you contain all the power in the world, that you are capable of everything, that you have wings. There is no more precious moment in life than this . . . and you will work very hard for years just to taste it again."

At the heart of deep play is a form of meditation favored especially by westerners; people who tend to prefer bustle to inertia prefer to meditate in motion. Meditation requires concentrating on a limited field; a rhythmic motion (usually deep breathing); repetition to clear the mind of distractions; withdrawal from the world; alert relaxation; mental cleansing or emptying; a release from previous habits and knowledge. In deep play, one also finds physical and mental control, sensory alertness, the ability to ignore pain. Both rely on focus, integration, and power; and both contain elements of self-hypnosis. With one's senses heightened, one enters "the zone," "the flow," a "cocoon of consciousness," in which one feels a strong sense of detachment from the relationships and trappings of ordinary life. *Detachment* is what we call it in the West, because we're so fixated on clinging to people and material things that we can only imagine being violently wrenched away from them. But Buddhists would call it *nonattachment,* a state in which craving to be elsewhere or otherwise or in possession of anything simply doesn't happen. They are two views of the same mental sanctuary. "I liken running," psychiatrist Thaddeus Kostrubala writes, "to one of the major techniques of meditation, and sometimes prayer, employed by virtually all disciplines East and West: the constant repetition of a particular word or series of words . . . the same process occurs in the repetitive rhythm of slow long-distance running. Eventually, at somewhere between thirty and forty minutes, the conscious mind gets exhausted and other areas of consciousness are activated."

As a reservoir of deep play, games, sports, religion, and art have much in common, and may even be interchangeable. "Games often create an order that resembles the cadenced life of ashrams and monasteries," Esalen's founder, Michael Murphy, writes, "and sporting expeditions are in certain respects like religious pilgrimages. . . . The spatial and temporal boundedness of sport, by ordering and sublimating our energies and by closing off the world's drudgery and confusion, can evoke our spiritual depths like a work of art or a monastic discipline."

Deep players are ascetics who withdraw from the world for a while and enter a meditative state. This state may be active, even full of commotion, but the player often reports a sense of calm and well-being. When playing golf, for example, one strolls over undulating lawns at a slow pace, in relative quiet, even when the stakes are high. "I'd liken it to a sense of of reverie," Arnold Palmer writes about his mood during tournament play, "not a dreamlike state but the somehow insulated state that a great musician achieves in a great performance. He's aware of where he is and what he's doing, but his mind is on the playing of his instrument with an internal sense of *rightness*—it is not merely mechanical, it is not only spiritual; it is something of both, on a different plane and a more remote one." As I said, some activities are more conducive to deep play than others, but what matters is the mood, not the activity. One can hunt mushrooms with an enthusiasm bordering on mania, find bliss in building a wall of perfectly balanced fieldstone, lose the world while performing complex surgery. Deep play can be solemn or rich with laughter.

On the other hand, one can turn bronco riding into drudgery. One can create mildly. One can live at a low flame. Most people do. We're afraid to look foolish, or feel too extravagantly, or make a mistake, or risk unnecessary pain. You'd think there was a golden ledger in the sky on which debits and credits were carefully noted, a scale on which each thought and action was assayed. For some, life is an exercise in moderation. The best china is saved for special occasions and thus rarely enjoyed. One fears intensity. But, given something like death, what does it matter if one looks foolish now and then, or tries too hard, or cares too deeply? A shallow life creates a world flat as a shadow. In that half-light, the sun never burns, risks recede, safety becomes habit, and individuals have little to teach one another. "The waking have one common world," Homer observes, "but the sleeping turn aside each into a world of his own." Westerners may prefer active states of meditation, but one can also reach deep play while sitting still—at a computer, for instance—without losing any religious devotion or flights of ecstasy.

As fresh technologies bloom, we should expect existing forms of worship to change dramatically and new religions to emerge. We may think of religion as a conservative force resistant to fad or change, but religions have always finessed the latest technology. Each major step in technology has mutated our idea of worship. Thirty to forty thousand years ago, when cave painting was a strange new idea, the Cro-Magnons extended their idea of worship by depicting creatures and symbols on cave walls.

Around 3500 B.C., the Sumerians carved prayers in cuneiform characters on clay tablets. Around 100 A.D., while Egyptians praised the glories of Isis in hieroglyphs, the Essene Jews recorded the teachings of Jesus on papyrus scrolls. Around the first century A.D., when the first fragile books appeared, Christians combined and edited the holy scrolls into the codices of the Old Testament. While the Romans continued to read about their gods in unwieldy scrolls, the Christians embraced the new technology wholeheartedly; it meant that they could easily transport their religious teachings. The only drawback was that each page had to be created laboriously by hand, and, in time, medieval scriptoria were filled with monks illuminating copies of the Latinate Bible, which they illustrated profusely and bound in durable leather. The activity brought them mental illumination, as well; it became a form of meditation, prayer, and artistry. Only the elite could afford to buy such manuscripts in what was essentially "the first information age," as Martin Irvine has called it. "It was the first time a whole civilization [had] a standard technology for recording and distributing information." Then, in 1456, Johannes Gutenberg invented movable type and the printing press, choosing the Bible as the first example of this new technique. He only managed to print two hundred copies of the Bible, but that nonetheless revolutionized religion, whose teachings one could suddenly learn privately and at home. By 1500, there were nine million books in Europe, most of them religious works. Because of the printing press, the Bible could be mass-produced, but so could new interpretations of it, such as Martin Luther's. Thus religion began to evolve at speed, with new splinter groups, new dogma. Through the printed word, evangelists could reach and persuade multitudes. The invention of radio multiplied that power, and quickly became a pulpit for Sunday-morning sermons. When television swept America in the 1950s, it didn't take long for Billy Graham, Oral Roberts, and others to broadcast their faith. So many preachers now have taken to the airways that we've had to coin the word *televangelism* for the phenomenon.

What's next? God on the Internet. One can attend the First Cyberchurch of the Scientific God, the Aquarian Concepts Community Divine New Order Government, the First Internet Church of All, and hundreds of Protestant denominations. There is a website devoted to the Celtic religion, to Mormonism, to Jainism, and Tibetan Buddhism, and several for Asatru (if you wish to worship Thor and other Norse gods). Most surprising of all, perhaps, is finding an Amish website—I thought the Amish vigorously eschewed technology. Also represented is shamanism, Druidism, Voodoo, and paganism. Apparently, 500 people each day visit the pantheist website. Those who believe in Gaia can join others in worship, as can ecospiritualists. There are two websites for Cao Daiism, a curious Vietnamese sect that for some reason worships novelist Victor Hugo as saint. Many individuals have established their own websites, to celebrate their personal holiness and look for followers. As Robert Wright discovered, surfing the web for *Time,* one can

> ... enroll in the "Starseed Schools of Melchizedek" and perhaps arrange a "personal transmission" with "Gabriel of Sedona." Gabriel, by the way, carries the endorsement of the "head administrator of our universe" (the two of them "fuse" once a month) and, moreover, is "the only morontia counselor/soul surgeon on Urantia (Earth) at his level of healing ability." ... This website also offers you the chance to pay money for sacred texts, learn about "Ascension Science," even explore the "Deoatomic body;" or "tron therapy ..."

The Vatican has a website (you can E-mail the pope, a great fan of the Internet), as do many convents and monasteries, including those supposedly in desert isolation. God has 410,000 online sites.

Thousands of people debate religious dogma, read theological newspapers, and chat with members of their faith online. Parishioners expect their churches to be up-to-date, offering counsel appropriate to the technological era we live in. There aren't many places where the devout of different faiths can mingle in safety, discover similarities, and discuss conflicts.

Using the web to proselytize, the thirty-nine members of the Heaven's Gate group believed that a spaceship, hiding behind the Hale-Bopp comet, awaited their attendance. No transporter beams would carry them aloft; they had to die out of their mortal flesh to be resurrected among angelic aliens. "Hale-Bopp's approach is the marker we've been waiting for," they explained on their website. "We fully desire, expect and look forward to boarding a spacecraft from the Next Level very soon." According to their gospel, Christ was an extraterrestrial:

Two thousand years ago . . . upon instruction, a member of the Kingdom of Heaven then left behind His body in that Next Level . . . and moved into (or incarnated into) an adult human body (or "vehicle") that had been "prepped" for this particular task. The body that was chosen was called Jesus. . . . Remember, the One who was incarnated in Jesus was sent for one purpose only, to say, "If you want to go to Heaven, I can take you through that gate—it requires everything of you."

As exotic as some of these web faiths may sound, one has to remember that all religions began as cults. Practiced in secret, with a strong element of danger, they included special rites and ceremonies, and usually required costumes and music, sometimes dance. Followers turned to them for a sense of community and order, transcendence and truth, an escape from daily routine. They offered glorious opportunities for deep play. Thus new

religions are bound to emerge, and, if they're relevant and popular enough, they'll become respectable. Ecospirituality is on the
verge of doing that right now. Most religions that emphasize
transcendence separate the idea of soiled body and clean spirit.
They compel believers to regard life on Earth as foul, temporary,
and sinful to enjoy. Many religions repudiate Earth, urging the
faithful not to grow attached to it but to keep their sights on
Heaven. "The world is a marketplace we visit, the otherworld is
home," runs a Yoruba proverb from Nigeria. According to the
Bible, Earth's resources were designed for human exploitation. If
Earth is merely a shabby waiting room, why bother protecting it?
Wendell Berry warns where such a schism will lead us:

> By dividing body and soul, we divide both from all else. We
> thus condemn ourselves to a loneliness for which the only
> compensation is violence—against other creatures, against
> the earth, against ourselves.

Religions that encourage a loss of self are, in essence, encouraging
an acceptance of death during life, a conscious as-if of death, a relief from the struggles of self.

As jarring as Heaven's Gate's demoting the body to a "vehicle" may seem, it's not new. Nor is perceiving the body as a mere
vessel for the soul. This notion of the body as a bottle in which
consciousness is trapped like a genie appears in so many works
of art, and is central to so many philosophies and religions, that
it's clearly a fantastic sensory illusion all humans share. As
Csikszentmihalyi points out, it's a practical view: "From an evolutionary standpoint, the self is a very chancy mutation. Its ad-
vantages are clear: By acting as a clutch between programmed
instructions and adaptive behaviors, it enormously increases the
possibilities of a fit between the two." However, the illusion can
feel strange. Samuel Beckett described the body as a wheelbarrow

for the brain. Seventeenth-century philosopher René Descartes argued that the body had many parts but the mind was whole and separate. When I was a teen, I tried to draw what it looked like staring out at the world through my eyes, with a slight blur of cheek here, an edge of nose there. I never could quite capture it, but I think most people have experienced that same sensation, the illusion that their mind is locked up inside a fragile body. I say illusion, because what we call *mind* doesn't dwell entirely in the brain, but travels the body on a caravan of hormones and enzymes. We can picture an operator and what he operates, so we picture the brain operating the body like a marionette, but of course it isn't so. The brain is a dark, silent world filled with life-saving illusions. An editorial in *New Scientist* offers this one:

> A tennis player, for example, experiences hitting a ball long after the ball has flown back over the net, and a driver's emergency stop begins before conscious apprehension of the danger. Our brains keep the illusion of conscious control alive only by constantly "backdating" the chain of events so that they make sense.

Memory adds to the moment and makes it seem larger than when it happened, more meaningful or poignant. Some say that happiness is a phantom of memory, and the only paradise a remembered one. Certain memories can hurt at first and then slowly grow, accrete, provide one with a moral and spiritual substance, a wish to continue living.

Many religions teach that a holy spirit dwells in a profane body. If Heaven is what matters, why enjoy being alive? If the body is only a container, why respect it? Such teachings are usually accompanied by ideas of *pure* and *impure*. What is impure must be cleansed—that creates a need for further dogma, ritual, and religious leaders. This attitude may rely in part on a fear of women's sexuality. Although women originally dominated all three of the monotheistic religions, they quickly lost their status and in time were declared dirty. The origin of our word *bad* is the Old English word *baeddel,* which meant an effeminate man. Being born of woman, through women's genitals, was thought to corrupt a man. To this day, male initiation rites all over the world (including fraternities and the military) usually require a man to purge himself of female contamination. Why such an emphasis on the power of women to seduce and defile men? The toxic version of woman, identified with Eve, a fallen woman who lured a man to his doom, a woman whose very name sounds like the word *evil,* appears repeatedly throughout the Judeo-Christian tradition. Here's just one nasty example, from Father Odon, the abbot of Cluny Abbey, in 1100, who wrote:

> Indeed, if men were endowed, like the lynxes of Boetia, with the power of visual penetration and could see what there is beneath the skin, the mere sight of a woman would nauseate them: that feminine grace is only saburra, blood, humor, bile. Consider what is hidden in the nostrils, in the throat, in the belly: filth everywhere. . . . How can we desire to hold in our arms the bag of excrement itself?

The pure realm is heaven, the impure is Earth, the church is a sacred place connecting the two. But when a church exists only on the Internet, where is it located? What rituals and ceremonies can take place there? What do we mean by a virtual community? Temples and churches have traditionally provided a concrete, physical place where people go to socialize, offer aid, comfort one another. Now that the sacred grove exists as a mass hallucination hovering in cyberspace, how will our idea of a church change? How can it nourish as it used to? On the other hand, by reinstalling the mysterious, maybe it will appeal to multitudes. Even if we consider only the three major monotheistic religions, Judaism, Christianity, and Islam, most people believe in the existence of, and worship, an otherworldly entity. If you demystify a religious creed, then what's left? People need to feel there is something greater than self, something answerable to, a sense of being monitored. One purpose of religion is to teach the parameters of life in society and nature.

All games and religions impose an order on the world, a certain attitude that must be adopted, ethical codes, rules of conduct. Submission is always an element of such devotion, but so is the freedom to create, problem-solve in new ways, and take action to help oneself or others. Some countries have tried to retain the framework of religion, while replacing the role of god with that of state or motherland. Many scientists and philosophers have been rational atheists. Myself, I lean toward ecospiritualism, but heaven knows there are rabid folk in the environmental ranks, overly solemn people who know too much what nature is for to be able to enjoy it. Religious authority can be respected or ignored—but both attitudes seem to attract extremists.

Heaven's Gate was not alone in perceiving Hale-Bopp as a messenger. Offering hallelujahs on the Internet, a host of sects welcomed the comet as a heavenly sign. Depending on the website, the comet would change the course of history, offer a rendezvous with extraterrestrials, signal the destruction of the world, or herald the coming of the Messiah. *Carpe diem,* "seize the day," is the unstated motto of all deep players. But for night-prowlers, day-sleepers, bat-fanciers, and comet-trackers, *carpe noctem* might well be the battle cry.

One evening, as I was stationary biking, headset on and country music blaring, I heard a loud pounding over the music. Not a roof-pounding as of raccoons, or a ground-pounding as of earthquake, but a higher pitched, sharp, fist-upon-glass pounding coming from eye level in front of me. For a few moments I felt alarmed and puzzled, before I realized someone was knocking on the windows. Tearing off my headset, I hurried to pull back the curtain, and saw my neighbor, Persis—bundled up in coat, hat, and mittens—waving her arms and grinning. "COMET!" she yelled.

"I'll be right there!" I yelled back, and grabbed a hat, gloves, long coat, and a pair of binoculars before rushing outside to climb into her car. Bundled up in the back seat, her ten-year-old, Cornelia, was looking excited, despite being in the second week of pneumonia.

"Sorry to startle you," Persis said, "but the sky suddenly cleared and I realized the comet was going to be perfectly visible *right now*. I thought we should seize the moment."

"Okay." *Carpe noctem.* She was right. The star-encrusted sky loomed overhead, clear and cold with the bottom lip of the moon bright enough to shower light over the puddled stars of the Pleiades, the tilted Dipper, and a huge ensemble of constellations. Even with a naked eye and through a car window, the comet was visible as a cottony blur low on the horizon near Cassiopeia. But soon we were far from the town lights and driving into the loam-darkness of the farm night. Turning up a side road, we drove to a hilltop overlooking the lake, which glittered like a pool of bubbling oil in the moon dazzle.

"Wow! Look at that comet!" Cornelia cried, pointing to the rare visitor from the deep freeze of space. Silver tail swept back by the solar wind, it was a picture-perfect comet, a big frozen dirt ball, the stuff of astronomy textbooks. Formed about four million years ago with the sun and planets, Hale-Bopp cruises at 43,000 miles an hour through the distant reaches of the solar system. Approaching Earth, it develops a few sparkling fountains as its water vapor, dust, and gases fume in the sun. Because we live by poetry, we call them tails. Some scientists believe that life on Earth owes its origin to comets—large snowballs the size of houses—which, over millions of years, rained down upon our planet with the building blocks of life, and enough water to form the oceans. More distant than those, Hale-Bopp is a radiant bypasser.

"Just imagine," Persis said, "it's only twenty-five miles wide. And 122 million miles from Earth." I've always relished Persis's elasticity. As a high-energy physicist, she happily studies the minute corridors of matter, where one is guided not by the particles themselves but by the trails they leave. Yet she's just as enthusiastic about large, blusteringly physical comets.

"How is that possible," I mused, "to be so small, so far away, and yet streak across the sky with such a brilliant light and diaphanous tail? How can we see it?"

Neither poet nor physicist knew. But Cornelia said she dreamed of riding on the comet, as if it were an icy white pony with a long tail. She seemed to be rubbing her sleepy eyes hard, but no, she was just focusing the binoculars. "Or maybe a dolphin," she added, imagining the dark sea of the sky, "or a unicorn." I scanned the heavens, but *delphis* was not yet visible. I could understand the pony's appeal, and the dolphin's, but how did our culture start playing so obsessively with the idea of unicorns?

In the fifth century B.C., Ctesias of Cnidus, a Greek physician to the Persian kings Artaxerxes II and Darius II, told of animals that have "a horn in the middle of the forehead"; powdered, the horn could make one "immune to poison." Unicorns were already legendary in China, ever since a particularly elegant and otherworldly one supposedly walked through the palace of Emperor Huang-ti in 2697 B.C. Throughout the western world, unicorns adorned tapestries, carvings, paintings, and jewelry. Its magical horn was reputed to cure most illnesses, and, more important for kings and queens, detect and neutralize poison. So

royalty often had eating utensils made of carved "unicorn horn."
When Catherine de Médicis became engaged to the dauphin of
France, Pope Clement VII gave him a gold-bedecked unicorn
horn as a wedding present, and, presumably, as a hint about dealing with Catherine. National debts could be paid off with unicorn
horns. Ivan the Terrible bought one horn for a small fortune and
made it his "staffe imperiall." The horn itself was not a fabulist's
dream. Something real was bought and sold. By all accounts, the
unicorn horn was pale, long, and tapered, twisting into a helical
spiral. So magical and mysterious was its origin that Leonardo
da Vinci, in his treatise on catching unicorns, suggested using
a virgin as bait. But by the end of the sixteenth century, when arctic exploration flourished, explorers discovered the truth about
unicorns. Narwhals, which live in arctic regions, grow long, tapered, spiraling tusks that exactly fit the description of unicorn
horns. They were most likely hunted by Inuits and traded to
Vikings, who merchandised them with great savvy and secrecy.
Creatures of powerful myth, they were a galloping mystery and
as otherworldly as comets.

Ever since the Industrial Revolution, our gods and mythic
creatures have tended to be technological. Looking up into the
arc of Corona Borealis (the Crown), I smiled hugely as I spotted
a faint bike and rider pedaling toward the North Star. It was Pol-
ish novelist Bruno Schulz who first christened this constellation
in *The Street of Crocodiles* (1940), celebrating the universal appeal of
cycling:

Oh, stellar arena of night, scarred by the evolutions, spirals
and leaps of those nimble riders; oh, cycloids and epi-cycloids
executed in inspiration along the diagonals of the sky, amid
lost wire spokes, hoops shed with indifference, to reach the
bright goal denuded, with nothing but the pure idea of cy-

cling! From these days dates a new constellation, the thirteenth group of stars, included forever in the zodiac and resplendent since then in the firmament of our nights: THE CYCLIST.

What would the Satawal navigators make of this comet? I wondered.

I love thinking about such things. Oftentimes, as they age, people shift some of their risk-taking from the physical to the mental. Risk and challenge still attract me, but the playing field is changing. These days, I often enter the high plateau that Abraham H. Maslow celebrates, where one feels the rapture of witnessing and appreciating.

As we get older, there's only so much novelty, surprise, and pure adrenaline rush the body can stand. Peak moments of deep play are explosive, and can lead to a violent sense of death and rebirth. Being shaken to the core by sudden ecstasy is hard on the nervous system. As they mature and age, risk-takers are less likely to pursue such steep thrills. Instead, they may feel "the less intense plateau-experience," which "is more often experienced as pure enjoyment and happiness, as, let's say, a mother sitting quietly looking, by the hour, at her baby playing, and marveling, wondering, philosophizing, not quite believing." Transcendence doesn't require a bobsled run or scaling Everest, it doesn't require a single, orgasmic, violently dramatic event. As Maslow reminds us, there is also the rich play of the high plateau "where one can *stay* 'turned on,' " the realm of emperor penguins and stargazing. But one does need to invite deep play into one's life. A lunchtime bike ride or violin sonata can be intense enough. For years, I gamboled from one adventure to another, some dangerous, all soul-stirring. Now I'm less impetuous—skirting death and being sidelined by injuries will result in that—but I save plenty of time for deep play, whose spellbinding clarity I relish.

"See the unicorn?" I asked Cornelia, pointing out the constellation. She looked politely, but her mind was on the once-in-four-millennia comet.

Hale-Bopp was entering the plane of the planets from a right angle, slicing through our solar system. "Once every four thousand years," Persis said in amazement. "Where will the earth be the next time the comet visits? Much of what we associate with civilization happened in the past four thousand years."

I suppose in the scope of cosmic time, four millennia is a flicker, but when I picture the comet's last tour of Earth, I'm struck by how different the planet would have seemed between visits. With each return, it briefly spotlights Earth and one chapter in the long chronicle of human endeavor. Some have compared Hale-Bopp to a time capsule, a pendulum, a metronome, the rings on an ancient sequoia, a searchlight, "snapshots of celestial seasons—ancient yesterdays, a distant tomorrow." Four thousand two hundred years ago, Earth was a dark planet without its now-familiar encrustations of city lights. The Egyptian pyramids were only four hundred years old, the plow was high technology in Europe, the Incas, Aztecs, and Mayans didn't exist. Neither did the idea of the city. The comet's appearance probably caused havoc on Earth. Regarded as doom stars, comets usually foretold change and disaster. Indeed, the word *disaster* comes from the Latin for "bad star." When comets appeared mysteriously to smear light across the heavens, it meant the gods were angry, and so wars were waged, empires fell, rulers died. Both Charlemagne's death and Julius Caesar's were blamed on comets.

With this new visit, the earth is lit like a sparkling jewel. There seem to be as many constellations on the ground as in the sky. Ignorance and unhappiness still rampage, humans and other animals still struggle for survival, lovers quake and yearn as they always did. But what a change in the complexion of human life, in the idea of transportation, communication, education, art, science, medicine. After all, we only began conquering diseases a century ago.

Sometimes I feel a vague sadness I can't touch or name. I carry it like a rod of light tucked under the calf muscle. When I realize that I won't be around for the comet's next passage, so many sadnesses fill my heart, fill it with a grief both ontological and particular. Curiosity about the future plagues me, but I will never again see this comet blaze across the sky. What will the comet witness in four thousand more years? Will Earth exist? Will humans? What truths will they have learned? Sixty thousand people are being born from dawn to dusk each day. Soon the earth will not be able to support its population. Where will they live? What will they eat and drink? Will beef, chicken, fish, and other corpse food be regarded as taboo? How will they find fuel to keep warm? Will they abandon Earth's surface, as Arthur C. Clarke predicts in *3001,* and build orbital cities fed by elevators towering up from the planet? What will they worship? Equally important: how will they play? For, as Ovid wrote millennia ago: "In our play we reveal what kind of people we are." This becomes especially true in our moments of deepest play—which is not always free of anxiety, but nonetheless great fun. Visionary, absorbing, ecstatic, extraordinary, deep play rapidly can become rewarding and healing, or dangerously addictive. Human nature being what it is, that will never change. Our daily routines tend to be haphazard and filled with work, chores, and requirements. How often do we shed all obligations and feel fully alive, freed from the identity we nonetheless cherish, as we use all our senses and become completely open to experience? Rarely. "We are vaguely wretched," Walter Kerr writes in *The Decline of Pleasure,* "because we are leading half-lives, half-heartedly, and with only one-half of our minds actively engaged in making contact with

the universe about us." When we allow ourselves to reach the
pinnacles of deep play, we become fully available to the world and
ourselves, out of context, beyond comparison, and in harmony
with life for a few glorious moments. Even when we climb down
from those heights, we carry with us some valuable skills and
insights. Deep play will always feel enthralling, but its details
may change as basic ideas like "control," "environment," "self,"
"body," "god," and countless others we now take for granted
begin to evolve.

Yes, I'm sure civilizations will still evolve through play, or
rather *as* play, since that seems to be a fundamental mechanism of
our humanity. New religions will arise, new art forms, new ways
to tantalize or jolt one's senses. Artists will continue to reveal
how the world touches us, how we are linked to the powerful
unseen forces of nature. For deep play, people will need sacred
arenas, rules, time limits, tension, exaltation, an openness to risk,
and the freedom to play. Of course, their versions of deep play
will explore new locales, new materials, new ways of evading the
grand concourse of society for a few rapturous moments.

But suppose paradise awaits us, as so many tales foretell—
freedom from disease, crime, early death. In a transcendent world,
what will become of our passion for transcendence? As efferves-
cent as turn-of-the-century life sometimes seems, we live in the
dark ages. I don't suppose those who lived before us thought of
themselves in the dark any more than we do, but it's inevitable:
the miraculous advances of each new age throw a shadow upon
the previous one. What discoveries, fascinations, and crazes we
will miss. I ache to see that future Earth, to know the triumphs
and struggles of those distant people, who will have other worlds
to conquer, other nights to cross.

There's a tradition of wishing on a falling star, but what does
one wish on a comet? For those future residents of Earth: may

their world still be packed with mysteries. May they still grow giddy on the eve of a great adventure. May they become more responsible to one another and to the planet. May they keep their taste for the renegade. May they never lose their sense of innocence and wonder. May they live to chase brash and astonishing dreams. May they return to tell me, if such a thing is possible, so that I can know the answers to a thousand scrupulous puzzles,

hear of whole civilizations that bloomed and vanished, learn what travel to other solar systems has revealed, and behold the marvels that arose while I was gone. If that's not possible, then I will have to make do with the playgrounds of mortality, and hope that at the end of my life I can say simply, wholeheartedly, that it was grace enough to be born and live.

Life is the game that must be played . . .
—Edwin Arlington Robinson,
"Ballade by the Fire"

Selected Bibliography and Notes

EPIGRAPH

vii "man is made God's plaything . . .": E. B. England, ed., *Laws* (New York: Longmans, Green & Co., 1921), pp. 803–4. Cf. also p. 685.

CHAPTER ONE
Deep Play

3 "It is an activity . . .": Johan Huizinga, *Homo Ludens* (Boston: The Beacon Press, 1955), p. 132.

5 "Even crows play. . . .": Jane E. Brody, "The Common Crow, Too Close for Comfort," *The New York Times,* May 27, 1997, pp. C1, C6.

5 "I sat one summer evening . . .": Wendell Berry, "The Body and the Earth:" in *Recollected Essays, 1965–1980* (San Francisco: North Point Press, 1981), p. 112.

6 Play "creates order . . .": Huizinga, p. 10.

9 "One thinks of Tolstoy . . .": Peter Marin, "Border Tribes," *Coevolution Quarterly,* quoted in Rob Schultheis, *Bone Games* (New York: Breakaway Books, 1996), p. 170.

11 "[t]he rules of warfare . . .": Huizinga, p. 173.

13 Young Masai men: James A. Swan, "Moranism," in *Sacred Places* (Santa Fe: Bear and Company, 1990), p. 32.

13 Native Americans have often used . . . : Schultheis, p. 125.

14 "Psychotherapy takes place . . .": D. W. Winnicott, *Playing and Reality* (New York: Routledge, 1982), p. 38.

14 British therapist . . . : Robin Skynner, "Squaring the Family Circle," *Observer Magazine* (London), February 14, 1988, pp. 60–62.

17 D. E. Berlyne, *Conflict, Arousal, and Curiosity* (New York: McGraw-Hill, 1960), p. 107.

17 Mihaly; Csikszentmihalyi, ed., and Isabella Selega Csikzentmihalyi, *Optimal Experiences* (New York: Cambridge University Press, 1995).

17 Karl Groos, *The Play of Man* (New York: Appleton, 1901).

18 "such customs must be rooted . . .": Huizinga, pp. 25–26.

18 "the stakes are so high . . .": Jeremy Bentham, quoted in A. Alvarez, *Feeding the Rat* (New York: Atlantic Monthly Press, 1988), p. 30.

19 Phyllis Greenacre, "Studies in Creativity," in *Emotional Growth,* vol. 2 (New York: International University Press, 1971), pp. 399–615.

19 "Tonight the moon is invisible . . .": Diane Ackerman, *The Moon by Whale Light* (New York: Random House: 1991), p. xiv.

21 "It isn't that I find danger . . .": Diane Ackerman, *On Extended Wings* (New York: Atheneum, 1985), p. 8.

23 Deep time: Sven Birkerts also uses the expression "deep time" in *The Gutenberg Elegies: The Fate of Reading in an Electronic Age* (New York: Fawcett Columbine, 1994), p. 75.

24 "One stands on the threshold . . .": Patsy Neal, *Sports and Identity* (Philadelphia: Dorrance and Co., Inc., 1972), pp. 90, 166–67.

25 "The person I became on Neva . . .": Schultheis, p. 12.

25 "messages of importance . . .": Charles Lindbergh, *The Spirit of St. Louis,* quoted in ibid., p. 19.

25 "there was no anxiety . . .": Albert von St. Gallen Heim, *Remarks on Fatal Falls,* quoted in ibid., p. 18.

26 "You feel a calmness . . .": Malcolm Smith, quoted in Michael Murphy, *The Psychic Side of Sports* (Reading, MA:, Addison-Wesley, 1978), p. 14.

CHAPTER TWO

At-One-Ment

27 "The bicycle, the bicycle surely . . .": Christopher Morley, *The Romany Stain* (New York: Doubleday, 1926), p. 42.

29 "The evil of the action . . .": Rudolf Otto, *The Idea of the Holy* (New York: Oxford University Press, 1923), p. 55.

31 "it amounts to a ritual . . .": Benjamin DeMott, "An Unprofessional Eye . . . Suspended Youth," *American Scholar,* vol. 32 (Winter 1962–63), pp. 107–112.

32 "The flesh becomes light . . .": Isadora Duncan, *The Art of the Dance* (New York: Theatre Arts, 1928), p. 51.

32 "When she danced . . .": ibid., p. 23.

32 "they make use of red-hot irons . . .": John Porter Brown, *Darvishes: Or Oriental Spiritualism,* 2d ed. (London: Frank Cass Co., 1968), p. 281.

37 Atop Everest . . . : footnote in Jon Krakauer, *Into Thin Air* (New York: Villard Books, 1997), p. 128.

46 "To halt and hang . . .": Jacques-Yves Cousteau with Frederic Dumas, *The Silent World* (New York: Harper and Row, 1958), p. 6.

46 In Shark Bay . . . : dolphin study reported by Rachel Smolker, *Ethology*, vol. 103, (1997), p. 454.

CHAPTER THREE

Sacred Places

49 "There are no more deserts . . .": Albert Camus, *Lyrical and Critical Essays* (New York: Vintage Books, 1970), p. 109.

49 "The perfect stillness . . .": William James, *The Varieties of Religious Experience* (Boston: Mentor Books, 1902), p. 57.

50 "Regardless of the words . . .": Bruce Chatwin, *The Songlines* (New York: Penguin USA, 1987), p. 108.

51 "Aborigines have a special connection . . .": Gulawarrwuy Yunupingu and Silas Roberts, chairmen of the Northern Land Council, statement in IWGIA (International Work Group for Indigenous Affairs), Document No. 54, *Land Rights Now* (Copenhagen: IWGIA Publications, 1967), p. 4.

53 "How can Mr. Court . . .": Fred Forbes, chairman of the Ngaanyatjara Council, in Daniel Vachon and Philip Toyne, "Mining and the Challenge of Land Rights," in Peterson and Langton, *Aborigines, Land and Land Rights* (Canberra: Australian Institute of Aboriginal Studies, 1983), p. 307.

53 The same is true . . . : a more detailed account of the Lascaux cave paintings may be found in Diane Ackerman, *A Natural History of Love* (New York: Random House, Inc., 1994), pp. 216–17.

55 And what of the painters?: For more about what the lives of those ancestors may have been like, especially their ability to love, see the final pages of Ackerman, *A Natural History of Love.*

57 In the Black Hills . . . : for references to the Lakotas in sacred meadows and to the Chumash Indians, see Swan, p. 21.

62 "[t]he feeling of it . . .": Otto, p. 12.

64 "I thought I had never been . . .": Laurens van der Post, *Journey into Russia* (New York: William Morrow, 1964) p. 229.

64 The Lakota Indians . . . : The Lakota Indian word *skanagoah* ("the still, electrifying awareness one experiences in the deep woods"—Pam Colorado), from *New Voices from the Longhouse*, ed. Joseph Bruchac (Greenfield Center, NY: Greenfield Review Press, 1989), p. 77.

73 "The great lesson from the true mystics . . . :" Abraham H. Maslow, *Religions, Values, and Peak Experiences* (New York: Viking, 1970), p. 28.

79 "The mountains, each inside the other . . .": George Seferis, *A Poet's Journal,* trans. Athan Angnostopoulos (Cambridge, MA: Harvard University Press, 1974), p. 28.

CHAPTER FOUR

Into the Death Zone

81 "These games will be the death of me yet . . .": Schultheis, p. 41.

84 "Sport is not an escape . . .": A. Guttman, quoted in Csikszentmihalyi, p. 53.

87 "A bicycle also is an amulet . . .": Morley, p. 172.

89 Steve McKinney . . . : The information on Steve McKinney is drawn in part from his obituary, "Life of Velocity," by Peter Sheldon, *Outside,* February 1991, p. 20, and from Murphy, *The Psychic Side of Sports.*

90 Two independent studies . . . : "Gene Tied to Excitable Personality," *Science News,* vol. 149, January 6, 1996, p. 4. This article also cites the work of Robert Cloninger of Washington University School of Medicine in St. Louis.

92 "Only he who has attained the summit . . .": Marco Pallis, *The Way and the Mountain,* p. 32, quoted in T. C. McLuhan, *The Way of the Earth* (New York: Simon & Schuster, 1994), pp. 250–51.

93 "Walking on water . . .": Jack Kerouac, quoted in Schultheis, p. 71.

96 "If this stillness . . .": Yukio Mishima, *Sun and Steel* (Palo Alto, CA: Kodansha International, 1970), pp. 1–2.

CHAPTER FIVE

The Gospel According to This Moment

103 "people who spend . . .": Flann O'Brien, *The Third Policeman* (New York: New American Library, 1967), p. 48.

104 "In play we see . . . ": The Reverend Dr. Douglas J. Green, "Praying as Playing," sermon delivered at the First Congregational Church, Ithaca, NY, October 8, 1995.

106 "The experience of the holy . . .": Maslow, pp. 30–31.

108 "One of the reasons why religion . . .": Karen Armstrong, *A History of God* (New York: Ballantine Books, 1993), p. 4.

109 "School Prayer": Diane Ackerman, *I Praise My Destroyer* (New York: Random House, Inc., 1998), p. 3.

110 I remember when I . . . : Diane Ackerman, *The Planets: A Cosmic Pastoral* (New York: William Morrow & Co., 1976).

114 "Above the comforts . . .": Krakauer, p. 136.

115 "they have wagered . . .": Camus, p. 81.

115 "a land where everything . . .": ibid., p. 86.

Chapter Six
Creating Minds

133 "When the spirits are low . . .": Sir Arthur Conan Doyle, *Memories and Aventures* (Boston: Little, Brown & Co., 1924), p. 210.

133 "the bicycle is the noblest invention . . .": William Saroyan, *The Bicycle Rider in Beverly Hills* (New York: Ballantine Books, 1952), p. 53.

134 "his eternal friend . . .": Henry Miller, "My Bike & Other Friends," *Book of Friends,* Vol. 2 (Santa Barbara, CA: Capra Press, 1978), pp. 105–110.

134 "A few people . . .": Alfred Jarry, "The Passion Considered as an Uphill Bicycle Race" (1900), in Roger Shattuck and Simon Watson, eds., *The Selected Works of Alfred Jarry* (New York: Grove Press, 1965), np.

A French author and physician, Jarry invented "Pataphysics," which he described as a realm far beyond metaphysics that justified his carrying a gun, drinking absinthe, and riding a Clérmont Luxe bicycle, among other curious habits.

135 "How can I convey . . . ?": O'Brien, p. 72.

137 One example of that phenomenon . . . : Magic Eye doors exist because researchers figured out how the eyes of crabs worked, and were able to construct mechanical ones that could be used for doors.

Chapter Seven
The Ceremonies of Innocence

143 "We die containing a richness . . .": Michael Ondaatje, *The English Patient* (New York: Alfred A. Knopf, 1992), p. 261.

Chapter Eight
The Healing Power of Nature

155 "To have no consciousness . . .": Luigi Pirandello, "Sing the Epistle" (*"Canta l'Epistola"*), trans. Frederick May (London and New York: Oxford University Press, 1963), np.

160　in a Zenlike trance . . . : In *Bike Cult* (New York: Four Walls, Eight Windows, 1995), David B. Perry has this to say about Buddhism and bicycles: "To his followers, Buddha (c.563–483 B.C.) was the Wheel King who rolled over the whole world with his footprints showing two bicycle-like lotus wheels, and created the Wheel of Law, Truth and Life, with the Round of Existence."

164　the Michaux Cycle Club . . . : Pryor Dodge, *The Bicycle* (New York: Flammarion/Abbeville, 1996), p. 155.

167　"The performance of the most informal . . .": Brother Joseph Keenan, in Mardawn Wendt's "The Art of Taking Tea," *Wombats News,* August 1997, p. 3.

170　"The song-maker draws inspiration . . .": This quote was taken from pp. 171–72, Vol. 10, *The Kwakiutl,* of Edward S. Curtis's twenty-volume *The North American Indian.* This monumental work, which Curtis began in 1907 in Seattle and completed in 1930, set out to document, in words and photoengravings taken from his glass-plate negatives, over eighty tribes west of the Mississippi. It was partly financed by J. P. Morgan, edited by Frederick Webb Hodge, and sponsored by President Theodore Roosevelt, who also contributed an introduction to the series.

CHAPTER TEN

The Night of the Comet

189　"Some things turn me on . . .": Smoke Blanchard, quoted in Michael J. Apter, *The Dangerous Edge* (New York: The Free Press/Macmillan, 1992), p. 34.

189　"I grow less and less afraid . . .": Colette, *Earthly Paradise,* ed. Robert Phelps (New York: Farrar, Straus and Giroux, 1996), Part Six (1939–1954), p. 501.

194　"while the blood is pounding . . .": Yuri Vlasov in Robert Lipsyte, *Sportsword* (New York: Quadrangle Books/New York Times Book Company, 1975), p. 280.

195　"I liken running . . .": Thaddeus Kostrubala, *The Joy of Running* (Philadelphia: J. B. Lippincott Co., 1975), p. 103.

195　"Games often create . . .": George I. Brown and Donald Gaynor, "Athletic Action as Creativity," *Journal of Creative Behavior,* vol. 1, no. 2 (1967), pp. 155–52. Quoted in Murphy, *The Psychic Side of Sports,* p. 119.

195　"I'd liken it to a sense of reverie . . .": Arnold Palmer, *Go for Broke* (New York: Simon & Schuster, 1973), p. 141.

198　"enroll in the 'Starseed Schools . . .' ": Robert Wright, "Can Thor Make a Comeback?," *Time,* December 16, 1996, pp. 68–69.

199 "Two thousand years ago . . .": David A. Kaplan, "The Return of the Great Comet," *Newsweek,* March 24, 1997.

200 "By dividing body and soul . . .": Wendell Berry, "A Native Hill," in *Recollected Essays,* p. 112.

200 "From an evolutionary standpoint . . .": Csikszentmihalyi, p. 21.

201 "A tennis player . . .": editorial in *New Scientist,* April 5, 1997, p. 3.

202 "Indeed, if men were endowed . . .": Odon of Cluny, quoted in Jean-Paul Sartre, *Saint Genet,* trans. Bernard Frechtman (New York: George Braziller, 1963), p. 78.

206 "Oh, stellar arena . . .": Bruno Schulz, *The Street of Crocodiles,* trans. Celina Wieniewska (New York: Penguin Books, 1977), p. 134.

208 "snapshots of celestial seasons . . .": Kaplan.

Acknowledgments

Some thoughts about the importance of poetry, ceremony, and ecopsychology are loosely based on essays entitled "The Value of Poetry," "The Ceremonies of Innocence," and "The Healing Power of Nature," which appeared in *Victoria*.

My interest in Gauguin led me to visit the Marquesas and write about the journey for *Travel-Holiday,* while some of my musings about the grandeur of the Grand Canyon first appeared in *Harvard Magazine.*

The two short passages about ballooning and *Symbion pandora* began as Op-Ed pieces for *The New York Times.*

Index

BOOKS BY DIANE ACKERMAN

DEEP PLAY

Ackerman introduces the state of transcendence she calls deep play, a state of unselfconscious engagement with our surroundings that draws from us our finest performances and taps into the faculties that make us feel most fully alive. She shows us that understanding deep play, and some of the ways it is attained, is understanding how lives filled with joy, creativity, and self-fulfillment are sustained.

Nonfiction/0-679-77135-2

I PRAISE MY DESTROYER
Poems

Divided into seven sections, including "Timed Talk," "By Atoms Moved," and "Tender Mercies," *I Praise My Destroyer* is less an assorted poetry collection than an organically coherent whole, one that reveals Ackerman's true calling as a twentieth-century metaphysical poet of the highest order.

Poetry/0-679-77134-4

JAGUAR OF SWEET LAUGHTER
New and Selected Poems

Ackerman's Olympian vision records and transforms landscapes from Amazonia to Antarctica, while her imaginative empathy penetrates the otherness of hummingbirds, deer, and trilobites. Her poems are indelible reminders of what it is to be a human being—the "jaguar of sweet laughter" that, according to Mayan mythology, astonished the world because it was the first animal to speak.

Poetry/0-679-74304-9

THE MOON BY WHALE LIGHT

Whether she's sexing an alligator barehanded or coaxing a bat to tangle in her hair, Diane Ackerman goes to unique—and sometimes terrifying—extremes to observe nature at first hand. Provocative, celebratory, and wise, *The Moon by Whale Light* is a book that forges extraordinarily visceral connections between the reader and the natural world.

Nature/0-679-74226-3

A NATURAL HISTORY OF LOVE

From aphrodisiacs in ancient Egypt to Sigmund Freud, from Abelard and Heloise to *Blade Runner*, the poet and naturalist delivers an exuberant, scientific, anecdotal tour of the "great intangible"—love in its many forms.

Nonfiction/0-679-76183-7

A NATURAL HISTORY OF THE SENSES

In the course of this grand tour of the realm of the senses, Ackerman tells us about the evolution of the kiss, the sadistic cuisine of eighteenth-century England, the chemistry of pain, and the melodies of the planet Earth with an evocativeness and charm that make the book itself a marvel of literate sensuality.

Nonfiction/0-679-73566-6

THE RAREST OF THE RARE
Vanishing Animals, Timeless Worlds

With the insatiable curiosity and lavish powers of description that have made her our foremost naturalist-poet, the author journeys in search of monarch butterflies and short-tailed albatrosses, monk seals and golden lion tamarin monkeys: the world's rarest creatures and their vanishing habitats. She delivers a rapturous celebration of other species that is also a warning to our own.

Nature/0-679-77623-0

A SLENDER THREAD

In this intimate and compassionate record of her service as a counselor on a suicide and crisis hotline, Ackerman turns her attention to the troubled lives of those suffering from what she calls the "small demonology of our age"—anxiety, depression, and all the trials, uncertainties, and conflicts of love.

Nonfiction/0-679-77133-6

VINTAGE BOOKS
Available at your local bookstore, or call toll-free to order:
1-800-793-2665 (credit cards only)

Printed in the United States
by Baker & Taylor Publisher Services